O'SHAUGHNESSY LIBRARY

This book is presented to you
with the compliments of
Rosemount Inc.,
Eden Prairie, Minnesota,
and Mr. Vernon H. Heath,
Chairman and Chief Executive Officer

Courage Center • 3915 Golden Valley Road • Golden Valley, Minnesota 55422

COURAGE
The Story of Courage Center

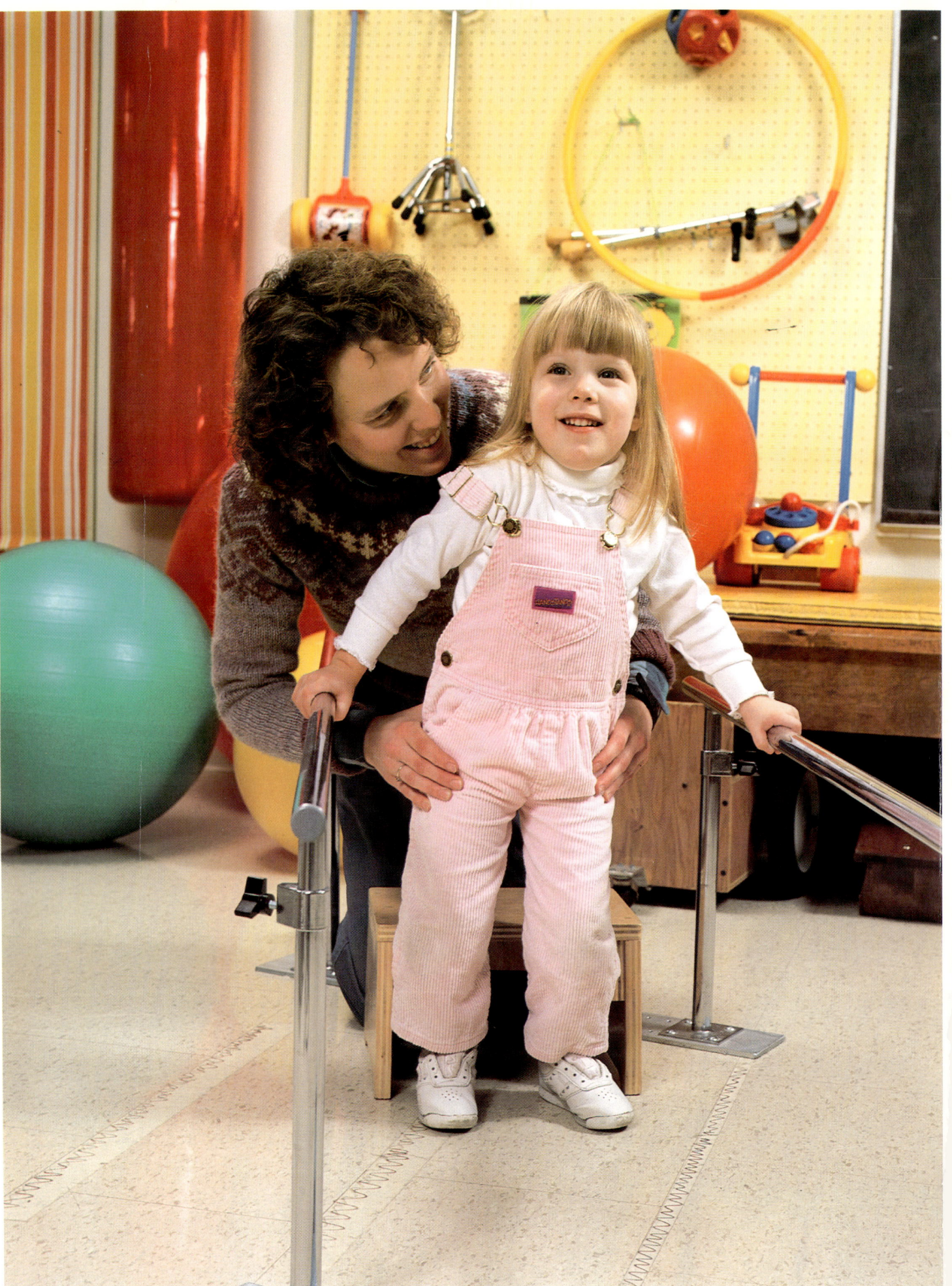

COURAGE

THE STORY OF COURAGE CENTER

Mavis A. Voigt

Courage Center • Golden Valley, Minnesota • 1989

Project Director: Wilko B. Schoenbohm
Managing Editor: E. B. Green
Design: Donald K. Skoro
Indexing: Suzanna Moody
Printer: Sexton Printing, Inc.

Frontispiece: Physical therapist Jodi Roos lends a steadying hand as Nicole Tufenk of Bloomington practices walking.

All cities and towns mentioned are in Minnesota unless they are major cities or are otherwise identified. Photographs are from the Courage Center collection or by Courage Center staff photographers, including Lyle Davies, Steve Larson, Candy Jackson, Liza Fourré, and Terri Poehls, with these exceptions: Robert and Loren Paulson of North Star Photography donated their services for photographs on frontispiece and pages xii, 8, 63 (pool), 72, and 87; reproduced with permission from the Minnesota Historical Society, pages 10, 11 (figure), 12, 13, 16, 17; by Jeff Grosscup, pages 2 (lobby), 58, 59; by Joe Rossi of the *St. Paul Pioneer Press Dispatch,* page 5; by Phillip and Judy Sublett of the *Annandale Advocate,* page 18; by Donald Black of the *Star and Tribune, Newspaper of the Twin Cities,* page 23; by J. W. Franklin, page 25 (ABC); by Don Walter, page 39; by Sinkler Photography, page 62 (top); by Clarissa Uemura, page 66; by Bruce Bisping of the *Star and Tribune,* page 86; by Phillip M. James, courtesy of Rafferty, Rafferty and Tollefson (architects), page 97 (atrium); courtesy of Dorothy Prichard, page ll (portrait); and courtesy of Jay Phillips, page 102.

Included in the author's sources were personal interviews, organizational newsletters and records, the records and collections of the Minnesota Historical Society in St. Paul, and books including James Haskins, with J. M. Stifle, *The Quiet Revolution* (New York: Thomas Y. Crowell, 1979); Gilda Berger, *Physical Disabilities* (New York: Franklin Watts, 1979); Nancy M. Crewe, Irving Kenneth Zola, and Associates, *Independent Living for Physically Disabled People* (San Francisco: Jossey Bass Publishers, 1983); C. Esco Obermann, Ph.D., *A History of Vocational Rehabilitation in America* (Minneapolis: T. S. Denison & Company, Inc., 1965); Ruth A. Velleman, *Serving Physically Disabled People* (New York: R. R. Bowker Company, 1979); and Frank Bowe, *Rehabilitating America* (New York: Harper & Row, 1980).

© 1989 by Courage Center, 3915 Golden Valley Road, Golden Valley, Minnesota 55422 (612) 588-0811
Library of Congress Catalog Card Number: 89-60274
ISBN 0-9622455-0-X
Manufactured in the United States of America

Dedicated to all those with disabilities who have shared their concerns, aspirations, and needs, without which the Courage story could not have been told

to all those who have responded to these needs by giving their time, talents, and means to make Courage facilities and services possible

and to those who have taken these means and molded them into a healing ministry, manifesting a spirit of love and compassion as they seek to improve the quality of life for us all

Contents

Foreword	IX
Preface	XI

Part One: A Community of Courage — 1

Part Two: The Courage Story — 9

1. Roots — 9
2. Early Efforts — 13
3. Camping: An Experiment — 17
4. A New Name and a New Focus: Rehabilitation — 21
5. Camp Courage — 27
6. Removing Barriers and Gaining Independence — 35
7. Mergers and Affiliations — 41
8. The Courage Center Dream Comes True — 49
9. Courage Residence — 51
10. Courage North — 55
11. Decade of Growth — 57
12. New Programs for Changing Needs — 65
13. Winds of Change — 73
14. Courage St. Croix — 83

Part Three: A Caring Community — 85

1. A Voluntary Tradition — 85
2. A Sharing Community — 93
3. Special Events and Visitors — 101
4. Looking Ahead — 107

Index — 108

Foreword

The doctor said "polio." An eight-year-old boy in a small farming community before the age of television, I had never heard that strange word. The aftermath of the diagnosis proved it to be grim. At the time the only polio patient in Princeton, I was to live at first in an isolated world. Later, in 1944, I had the opportunity to go to an early Courage camp as a teenager. On the St. Croix River near Hinckley, it was called "Head of the Rapids."

The Courage organization back then was small and lacking in resources. It was, however, motivated by its leaders to bring disabled people together, not just for fun and games, but to see the world from a different perspective, to learn that individuals with disabilities need not be isolated. They could be and were people who lived in society, enjoying fruitful lives and contributing to their own welfare and that of others.

At Head of the Rapids I met people like Marvin Thompson, who was pursuing a doctorate in English from a wheelchair, and Dick Olson (now known as Uncle Al), who had a broad view of life. They urged me to reach out farther than I had ever dreamed. I went to camp for four years, two weeks each summer, receiving encouragement that led me to seek new horizons, and I found a way to go to the University of Minnesota, earn a degree, and begin a productive life.

Since then I have watched Courage emerge from a small organization into one that, while maintaining its purpose—to help people help themselves—has developed great capability and resources to help carry out its mission. This took real vision and missionary zeal. And from over 40 years of observation, I recognize that Wilko Schoenbohm provided, over a long period, the dedication and relentless drive necessary to achieve Courage Center's goals.

Never has an organization been so well named as Courage. Never has an organization had a more noble purpose. Few organizations have changed and enriched the lives of so many. Today, for instance, I think of the happy smile of Chris Harmon, a son of one of our employees, whenever he is asked about the summers he's spent at Camp Courage.

We all need the courage that many of us have been fortunate enough to find through this organization that goes beyond nice-sounding words. All who have been touched by Courage Center will be delighted that its history is being preserved with this book.

VERNON C. HEATH
Chairman and CEO, Rosemount Inc.

Preface

In 1988 Courage Center marked 60 years of service to people with physical disabilities. The organization both shaped and was shaped by the events of those 60 years.

During the past year, we became involved in an effort to preserve the story of Courage Center, through oral interviews, research, and the compiling of a manuscript for this book. This work has been a labor of love both for me and for Mavis Voigt, an author and researcher associated with Courage Center as a staff member, volunteer, and friend for more than 30 years.

As the project has progressed, Mavis and I have been able to relive some wonderful experiences with people associated with Courage Center as clients, board members, volunteers, donors, and staff members. Without their willingness to share their stories, this history would not have been possible. We are grateful, too, to Courage Center's executive director, David Phillips, for encouragement and to those who provided funding: Rosemount, Inc., Eden Prairie, and its chairman, Vernon Heath, Edina; Mr. and Mrs. Jay Phillips, Minneapolis; the Baker Foundation, Minneapolis; the estate of William H. DeParcq, Tucson; Mr. and Mrs. John Hollern, Minneapolis; and the Casey Albert T. O'Neil Foundation, St. Paul.

Finally, I must acknowledge that my name and comments appear throughout the book much more often than I would like. I hope readers will understand that this is the result of my being executive director of the organization for more than 31 years, and that they will appreciate with me the timeless words of the Chinese poet, Lao-tzu:

A leader is best when he is neither seen nor heard;
Not so good when he is adored and glorified;
Worst when he is hated and despised.
"Fail to honor people, they will fail to honor you."
But of a good leader, when his work is done, his aim fulfilled,
The people will say, "We did this ourselves."

WILKO B. SCHOENBOHM

Part One
A Community of Courage

Visitors to Courage Center in Golden Valley, a western suburb of Minneapolis, consistently remark about two things: the positive spirit that prevails there and the involvement of people with disabilities on all levels.

What is remarkable is that the line between those who need and those who give at this major rehabilitation facility has blurred. Individuals with disabilities are a vital part of the rich fabric of Courage Center. They are clients to be sure, but they are also staff members, volunteers, teachers, and members of boards and committees, making decisions about Courage Center's future. Courage Center is truly a community of courage, a microcosm of an ideal society where individuals receive according to their special needs and give according to their special talents.

The story of Courage Center's development parallels that of the emergence of people with disabilities from the shadows of isolation and prejudice into the sunshine of life. It is the story of a revolution—a breaking down of barriers, both physical and attitudinal, and a building up of facilities and programs to help disabled individuals achieve independence and dignity.

The journey has not been easy. It has taken years of hope and planning and lifetimes of work and commitment. The vision that created Courage Center and guides its growth is the vision of America's founders of a better life for everyone, regardless of race, religion, economic status—or physical limitations.

The strength of Courage Center is in its creative leadership and strong public support. The organization proudly carries on a voluntary tradition begun by its founders and articulated by its former executive director, Wilko B. Schoenbohm, who said: "If the cause is right and the need is there, and you do a good job of describing the need, God and the American people—the most generous on the face of the earth—won't let you down."

The concerned citizens who founded the organization in 1928 could hardly have foreseen the scope of Courage Center services today. They would be amazed at the integration of individuals with disabilities into the mainstream of society and at the barriers that have fallen through the years. The organization's early goals were modest: to locate rural disabled children and help them get an education. They grew to include meaningful work for homebound disabled adults and provision of special equipment. Later goals embraced rehabilitation and activities that enriched lives, such as camping and recreation.

Early camping programs demonstrated that children with severe disabilities could enjoy a stay at a residential camp and grow tremendously from the experience. Later, adults too left their institutions and family homes for outdoor adventures. If disabled individuals could function so well in an accessible camp

Opposite: Pam Westling, receptionist for Courage Center's medical rehabilitation sevices, greets client Bonnie Marsh of St. Paul.

environment with caring staff, why could they not do so in the community? What was keeping them out of the mainstream? Old attitudes, fears, and prejudice, combined with inaccessible homes and workplaces and lack of transportation. Services such as special therapy, education, training, and recreation could help people function in the community, but the community itself had to change. Public buildings and facilities had to become accessible; sidewalks had to have curb cuts for wheelchairs; homes and public buildings had to be built without architectural barriers; workplaces had to be modified and transportation provided.

Many of these challenges are being met. Through a "quiet revolution," dramatic steps have been taken to open society to disabled individuals. Today, people with disabilities can study, work, enjoy leisure activities, compete in sports, marry, have families, live in accessible homes, and contribute their individual skills to American life. Courage Center plays a vital role in the continuing revolution—building facilities, launching programs and activities, influencing legislation, and educating the public about the needs and capabilities of people with physical disabilities and sensory impairments.

In carrying out its mission, Courage Center operates four debt-free major facilities in Minnesota:

Courage Center's lobby provides a comfortable, gardenlike setting for visitors and clients.

- The Courage Center headquarters in Golden Valley houses a transitional residence for young, severely disabled adults, a medical rehabilitation wing, a pool and gymnasium, administration and support services, and a broad variety of programs and activities designed to meet the physical, social, and emotional needs of individuals with disabilities.

Speech therapy center at Camp Courage

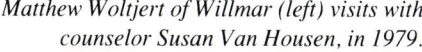

Matthew Woltjert of Willmar (left) visits with counselor Susan Van Housen, in 1979.

- Camp Courage, about 50 miles west of the Twin Cities, has two separate campuses on one site. One is for campers with physical disabilities and vision impairments, the other for children with speech and hearing impairments and language disorders. The site includes 35 buildings on approximately 300 acres, with about 5,000 feet of shoreline on two lakes.

Dining hall/recreation center for campers with physical disabilities at Camp Courage

Christopher Felt and his brother Jody, of La Crosse, Wisconsin, enjoy a cookout at Camp Courage, in 1971.

Molly Kenney of Anoka (left) and Phuonganh Nguyen of Excelsior share some experiences at Courage North, in 1980.

Leadership/dining hall at Courage North

- Courage North, a second residential camp, at Lake George, near Itasca State Park, offers a north-woods atmosphere, with log buildings on 95 pine-studded acres. Its programs stress outdoor adventures and leadership for hearing-impaired and physically disabled campers.
- Courage St. Croix, Courage Center's first satellite facility, opened in October 1988 in Stillwater, about 20 miles northeast of downtown St. Paul. It houses aquatic and therapy services and provides an outreach base, making Courage Center services available to people in the east metropolitan area, western Wisconsin, and the St. Croix River valley.

Courage St. Croix

All together, Courage Center offers more than 70 programs, each year benefiting some 22,000 children and adults with physical disabilities and speech, hearing, and vision impairments. Its services help meet the needs of individuals who have passed the stage of needing acute hospital care, who are medically and neurologically stable, and who can benefit from rehabilitation, independent-living programs, and recreational and enrichment activities. Services fall into these major program areas:

- Medical rehabilitation and education includes occupational and physical therapy, speech, language, and hearing services, children's services, psychosocial services, music and art therapy, life enrichment classes, equipment loan, and the Courage Stroke Network, a national organization of stroke support groups.
- Vocational services include evaluation, counseling, school and vocational placement, job readiness, and education for employers and citizens about the needs and abilities of employees with disabilities.
- Sports, physical education, and recreation programs offer recreational and competitive sports and lifetime fitness activities such as wheelchair basketball and square dancing, field and track, skiing, swimming, and special activities for individuals with hearing impairments.

Chad Miller of Woodbury enjoys the Courage St. Croix pool with the help of his volunteer "swim buddy," Maryn Scholl of White Bear Lake.

- Driver education evaluates and trains men and women with disabilities, enabling them to pass state driving examinations and become licensed drivers.
- Rehabilitation technology encompasses rehabilitation engineering, home modification services, and the international Courage HANDI-HAM System of amateur radio, with 7,000 members worldwide.
- Courage Residence, a transitional independent-living facility adjoining Courage Center, offers programs for young adults who are brain-injured, spinal-cord-injured, congenitally disabled, or severely disabled by injury or disease.
- Camping programs at Camp Courage and Courage North offer a variety of special sessions as well as regularly scheduled sessions for children and adults. In addition, Courage Center operates more than 30 day camps throughout the region.
- Volunteer services provide placement, training, and coordination for more than 1,200 volunteers working at Courage Center.
- The Courage Institute provides a forum for people with disabilities, caregivers, rehabilitation professionals, and the general public to share knowledge through seminars, research, and educational materials.

The scope of Courage Center services continues to broaden. Some programs, such as the Courage Stroke Network and Courage Residence, are national, and one, the Courage HANDI-HAM System of amateur radio, is international. Outreach programs including rehabilitation engineering, driver education, life enrichment, and sports and recreation continue to grow throughout Minnesota, Wisconsin, South Dakota, North Dakota, and Iowa, as Courage Center works to make services available to all who need them.

CATHY AND DEBBIE BURKE: MORE OPPORTUNITIES NOW

Cathy Burke, Minneapolis, has a scrapbook full of photos to help her remember Camp Kiwanis. Born in 1934 and disabled from osteogenesis imperfecta (brittle bones), she attended camp in 1947. It was her first experience away from both her family and the hospital where she lived as a child:

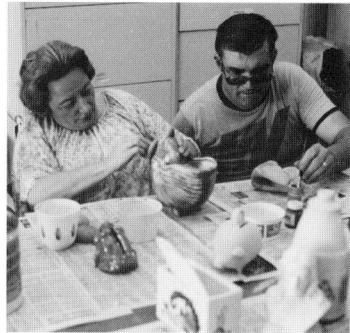

Cathy Burke and her husband, Bruce, enjoy a ceramics class at Courage Center, in 1979.

I had spent most of my life lying in a hospital bed, so camp was really an experience for me. I lived at Gillette State Hospital from 1938 to 1946, from age 4 to 12. We had a teacher who came to the bedside for 15 minutes a day. Of course, I had a lot of broken bones—138 of them by the time I left Gillette. In those days, they believed you should be immobile, so I was strapped onto a metal frame with traction on my legs. Sometimes during a thunderstorm I'd jump and the weights would bounce and break my leg. It was scary—I was only four years old and didn't have parents nearby to reassure me. They lived on a farm at the Minnesota-North Dakota border near Breckenridge and would come and visit me once a year.

When I came home from Gillette, I didn't remember my brother at all. He was one-and-a-half when I left, and my mother had three more children while I was in the hospital. I didn't know any handicapped people in the community, and I was quite isolated. Then my parents heard about Camp Kiwanis from the county nurse, and I started going there in 1947. It was a whole new world. I made new friends and we kept in touch all year. I loved the falls, and counselors carried me on their shoulders to the river, where I'd stay all day if I could. I loved the crafts and the archery. When I went to Camp Courage in 1956, I learned about how to get rehabilitation help so I could be more independent. After I got home, a Division of Vocational Rehabilitation counselor helped me go to business school, find a place to live, and get in touch with hearing services. Then, when I was 25, I got a job at a mailing service typing names on addressograph plates.

It all started at camp. I even met my husband, Bruce, at Camp Kiwanis, where he was a counselor. He had lost an arm and a leg in 1934, when he was hit by a train in Clarkfield. Our first daughter, Amy, was born in 1965. She does not have osteogenesis imperfecta, and our doctor said there was a good chance a second child wouldn't have it either. Debbie, born in 1970, does have it, but her life has been much different from mine.

Debbie Burke started attending Curative Workshop's therapeutic preschool in 1972, when she was two-and-a-half. When Courage Center opened, and the preschool moved, she transferred too. She attended Michael Dowling School until fourth grade, when she was mainstreamed part-time and then full-time. She attended public junior and senior high schools.

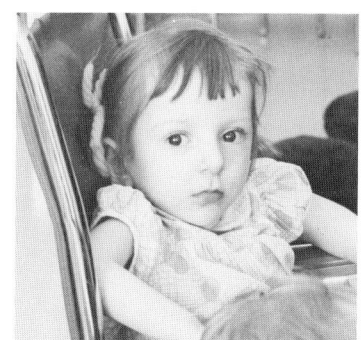

Debbie Burke in 1973

I liked Camp Courage a lot after I got used to being away from my parents. When I was seven and eight, I liked horseback riding and crafts best; when I got older I enjoyed my friends at camp the most. Being active carried over from camp to high school, where I earned three letters managing sports. I headed a disabled students' group and was in concert choir, the pep club, and on the student and senior councils. I was one of the royalty for homecoming at South High. I enjoyed school and really liked math and computers, and I tutored some kids in those subjects.

After graduating in the spring of 1988, I got a job at Metropolitan Community College, where I enrolled as a student in the fall. I had worked previous summers at the Lehmann Center and at Courage Residence as a weekend receptionist. After living three months in Courage Residence to learn some independent-living skills, I moved into an apartment with my girlfriend and hired an attendant I'd met at Camp Courage. I like being independent, and I know it's been easier for me to get there than it was for my mother. There are so many more opportunities now.

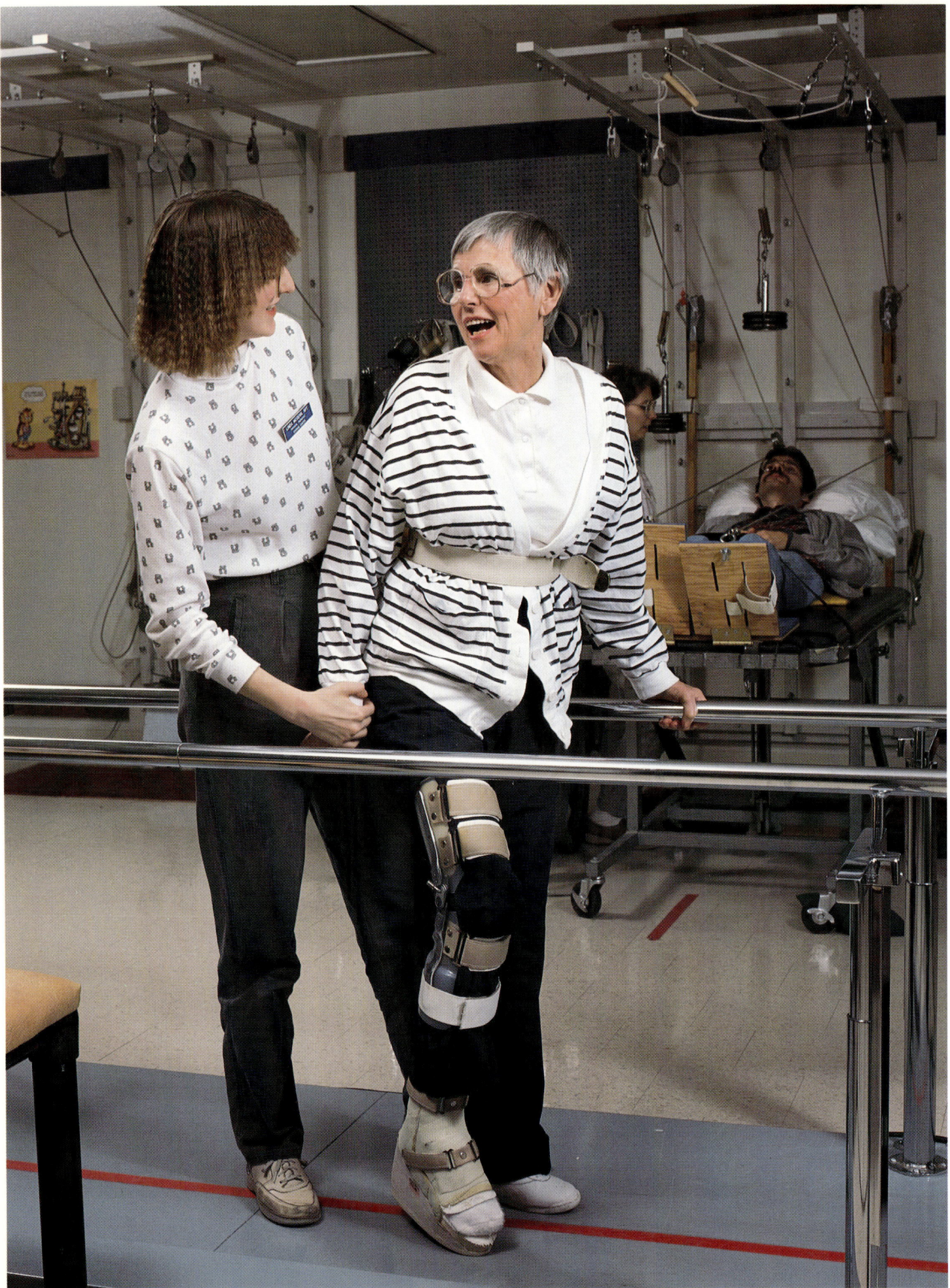

Part Two
The Courage Story

1 Roots

The organization that became Courage Center grew out of deep concern in the community for the plight of disabled children in Minnesota. Interested citizens had informal discussions on what should be done as early as 1921. Not until 1925, however, was the first formal conference organized. A group of leading citizens representing various agencies, clubs, schools, and hospitals gathered at the Nicollet Hotel in Minneapolis to discuss what they could do to help.

The conference was called by Oscar M. Sullivan, director of the State Division of Re-education, later known as the Division of Vocational Rehabilitation (now the Division of Rehabilitation Services). It was a remarkable grass-roots effort, reflecting a "crippled children's movement" throughout the nation. Carl C. Chatterton, orthopedic surgeon and later chief of staff of Gillette Children's Hospital in St. Paul, and C. E. Ovenshire, past Imperial Potentate of the Shrine, spoke to the group, alerting it to the needs of crippled children. Despite existing programs in the state, many problems were still not being adequately addressed.

Minnesota was already a national leader in showing concern for its disabled citizens. In 1897 its legislature had set aside funds for the first state-sponsored hospital for crippled children in the nation. Originally called the Minnesota State Hospital for Indigent, Crippled and Deformed Children, it was renamed Gillette Children's Hospital in honor of Arthur Gillette, the young orthopedic surgeon who helped establish it. The Minneapolis Board of Education had founded Michael Dowling School for children with disabilities in 1920, and the Twin Cities Shriners Hospital for Crippled Children had opened in 1923. In Duluth Kate Barnes had initiated a therapy program in 1922. No services existed for educating disabled children in rural Minnesota. So the participants in the 1925 meeting formed an embryonic organization called the Minnesota Conference for the Disabled, resolving to work voluntarily to "fill the needs of the handicapped not being met by public or private agencies and to pioneer in demonstrating further needs whenever or wherever they may exist."

In Ohio, another organization, guided by retired lumber magnate and Rotarian Edgar F. "Daddy" Allen, was taking shape. Allen's 18-year-old son, Homer, had been seriously injured in a streetcar accident on Memorial Day 1907. Because Elyria had no hospital and proper treatment was not available, the young man died. Allen turned his grief into a crusade, a dynamic force seeing through the construction of a hospital for Elyria and the establishment of a national organization with affiliates in every state, including the Minnesota Conference for the Disabled.

Through Allen's efforts, the Rotary clubs of several Ohio cities adopted a program to ensure that "the crippled child of Ohio shall have a fair chance and a

Opposite: Margaret Kusske of Roseville, aided by physical therapist Linda McGerr, works at regaining muscle strength after a stroke.

An early brochure of the Minnesota Association for Crippled Children quotes "Daddy" Allen.

square deal." The clubs founded the Ohio Society for Crippled Children in 1919, and the movement spread to clubs in other areas. In 1921 a federation of state organizations merged into the International Society for Crippled Children and Adults, later renamed the National Society for Crippled Children and Adults.

"Daddy" Allen spoke at the 1927 annual meeting of the Minnesota Conference for the Disabled at the Curtis Hotel in Minneapolis. He inspired the young organization with this message, printed on the program:

> In our work for crippled children we seek the sympathetic friendship of all who agree that human sympathy for human suffering is the motive spirit of Civilization. The accomplishment of this object, this hope and this aim is our desire, and we trust that the future will make it a reality in thousands of lives and hearts.

At the annual meeting, the organization changed its name to the Minnesota Association for Crippled Children. The group, formally incorporated on April 10, 1928, spelled out its ambitious goals in an early brochure:

> Save the Crippled Child—Reclaim the Adult: The plans of the organization are to locate all crippled children and disabled adults, to find out their needs, to enlist thousands of men and women as volunteers in giving the personal interest so necessary, to stimulate early hospitalization, convalescent care, and provision of schooling facilities and to promote the coordination of all existing efforts in the field. The Association will not duplicate any existing agency, but will supplement, guide, educate and arrange cooperation.

The Association, with headquarters at 11 West Summit Avenue in St. Paul, set its membership fee at one dollar, with life memberships for donors of $100 or more. Active, working committees could be members without paying a fee. Frank Hacking, M.D., of Minneapolis was the first president. One of the board members was Johanna "Jennie" Bordewich Dowling, widow of Michael J. Dowling, a leading citizen who despite great disabilities was an inspiration for the Association's founders.

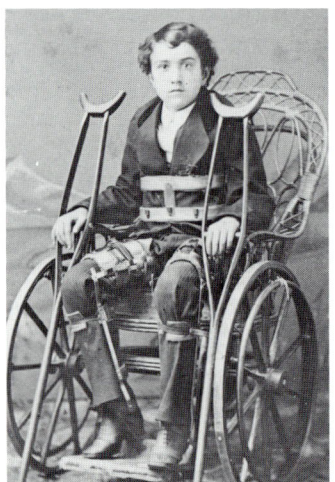

The late 1800s and early 1900s were bleak years for people with disabilities. This photograph carries one young man's message: "My name is Theophilus Webster Williams. I was born in Cambria, Columbus County, Wisconsin, in 1864. I have always been more weakly than other children of my age, and been growing worse, until now I am helpless, and wholly unable to do anything for myself, as I am troubled with spinal disease. I am selling my photographs to raise money to take me to the Infirmary at Indianapolis, and my parents having exhausted the little means that they had, I now ask your aid and sympathy; and our Heavenly Father will bless whatever you may give. Price, 25 Cents."

Michael J. Dowling: Think of What You Have

The Sultan of Sulu was bored, and his visitors knew it. They were there as emissaries of the U.S. government, so the sultan suffered their presence. They had to get his attention. Suddenly, one of the Americans grabbed his own left arm, tore it from his body, and tossed it on the floor. The sultan blinked, and the American reached first for his left leg, then for his right, pulling them away from his body and flipping them aside. The sultan gulped. When the American reached for his head as if it were next, the sultan rose quickly to his feet and begged him to stop, to share the secret of his magic. Michael Dowling had the sultan's attention.

Dowling was 14 when the blizzard of 1880 swept through Minnesota. The young cattle herdsman fell from the back of a lumber wagon near Canby and stumbled through the storm for hours, finally burrowing into a pile of straw, fighting to stay awake. In the morning when he tried to stand, he fell. His legs were frozen, and when he clapped his hands, "it was as if I had struck two blocks of wood together." Somehow, Dowling reached a nearby farmhouse, but 16 days later, without anesthetic, doctors amputated both his legs six inches below the knees, his left arm below the elbow, and most of his other hand. He said years later: "There were days when the future looked utterly black. Hardest to bear was the pity I received."

Dowling had supported himself from age 10, as a water carrier, a cowboy, and a cookee on the Mississippi steamers. Born in the Berkshire Hills of Massachusetts, he moved with his parents to Chicago and came to Minnesota alone when his mother died. Within a year after the amputations, his savings were gone. He sold his pony and the five head of cattle he'd purchased, and the townspeople made bandages for him by tearing up old pillow slips, sheets, and clothing. When in the spring of 1882 the county commissioners of Yellow Medicine County arranged to pay a local farmer two dollars a week to care for him, Dowling said, "That galled me." So he startled the board with a bold proposition: "If you will pay for one year at Carleton College, it will never cost this county another cent to keep me going as long as I live."

Outfitted with artificial limbs, Dowling attended Carleton College in Northfield, became an elementary school teacher, painted fences, ran a roller-skating rink, sold books and maps, became superintendent of the first high school in Renville County, published a weekly newspaper, married, had three children, and became president of the Olivia State Bank and the Minnesota Bankers Association. He traveled as an insurance agent, served two years as secretary of the National Republican League, visited the Philippines as a U.S. commissioner shortly after the Spanish-American War, became a state representative in 1901, and immediately took over as speaker of the house. Dowling rarely spoke of his disability, nor did he allow himself special privileges: "I knew if I treated myself as if I were different from other people, the world would follow my example."

"Don't spend your time thinking about the things that are gone and can't be brought back," he told disabled soldiers after World War I. "Think of what you have. Don't think you are a cripple because you've lost a limb or two. Keep your mind working and you can accomplish wonders." He traveled from hospital to hospital all over the country and became a worldwide spokesperson for the cause of people with disabilities. He spoke to huge throngs in New York and visited English hospitals for eight months at the invitation of the British government, astonishing his listeners by inviting them to rap on his wooden legs or squeeze his wooden arms.

Michael Dowling died in 1921 at age 55, but his message of hope served as an inspiration for generations.

—*Adapted from an article by J. Arthur Boschee, former director of communications for Courage Center*

Association members look on as Governor Floyd B. Olson signs the school transportation bill in 1931. Left to right are W. H. Ziegler, Association secretary-treasurer; Arthur E. Larkin, Association vice-president; Charles F. Englin and Mrs. Glenn Wyer, board members; Dorothy Jones, Eustis Hospital hostess; Oscar Sullivan, board member; and Senator John B. Pattison and Representative Harry Wahlstrand, sponsors of the bill.

2 Early Efforts

The time was right for the Minnesota Association for Crippled Children to take root and grow. Minnesota was young, vigorous, and prosperous, with great resources in lumbering and agriculture, and its citizens reflected a Yankee "can-do" attitude. With the return of 204,000 wounded veterans after World War I, the public was beginning to feel responsibility for helping people with disabilities become part of the community. For years, society had ignored individuals with disabilities, preferring to hide them away in homes or institutions. Now steps were needed to bring them out of their corners of isolation.

The Association focused on its tasks: to locate rural crippled children, build public awareness of needs, and develop demonstration projects that it hoped would eventually be carried out by public agencies. In 1919, Congress had enacted the Smith-Sears Vocational Rehabilitation Act, making the government responsible for educating and training disabled veterans. The act was extended to civilians in 1920, and the Minnesota Department of Re-education was established to carry out the law in the state. Medical professionals, as well as concerned citizens, initiated programs to help. In Minnesota in 1922 the junior board of the Visiting Nurse Association started an occupational therapy program for "shut-ins," with volunteers giving treatments, teaching crafts, and helping with daily living activities. This effort led to the establishment in 1931 of the Curative Workshop, which later merged with Courage Center.

Curative Workshop was the first outpatient physical therapy service in Minneapolis. The whole profession of physical therapy was new, the result of a merging of nursing and physical education techniques during the final days of World War I. In 1927, the Minnesota chapter of the American Physical Therapists Association was founded by 30 or so physical therapists from the ranks of registered nurses who worked with war veterans and poliomyelitis patients at the Mayo Clinic in Rochester.

A visiting nurse, ready to make her rounds, in 1925

The depression years following the stock market crash of 1929 were difficult for young voluntary organizations and for the nation. City streets teemed with the unemployed, and in Minneapolis labor unions marched and farmers demonstrated under the banner of the Farmers' Holiday Association, threatening a strike. When Governor Floyd B. Olson took office in 1931, statewide unemployment was at 20 percent—a staggering 70 percent on the Iron Range—and farm prices plummeted.

Despite the dark years of the depression, the Minnesota Association for Crippled Children pressed on to remedy some problems, particularly that of educating Minnesota's rural disabled children. "Every crippled child in school!" became the battle cry.

A Curative Workshop volunteer driver helps pick up and deliver children, in the 1940s.

Association members lobbied for change, and their efforts paid off in 1931 when Governor Olson signed a bill providing school transportation for rural disabled children. According to the Association's August 1932 newsletter, transportation was provided for 89 children the first year. Members also supported a bill passed in 1935 providing board and care for children living too far from schools with special classes, so they could attend school in nearby districts.

LORENA MCPEEK: THE CRIPPLED CHILD MUST BE EDUCATED

Lorena McPeek, executive secretary of the Minnesota Association for Crippled Children, wrote in a 1930 newsletter:

Let us center our attention upon the educational rather than the clinical solution of our problems . . . At a glance one might say the crippled children are cared for. But what about the liability of the child with no preliminary education? Can you imagine a crippled child attempting to go a couple of miles through snow on one foot and crutches? . . . We must see the whole problem from babyhood to adult life. We will then realize that the crippled child must be educated as well as hospitalized.

The Association piloted the first homebound teaching program in the state, providing special teachers and later home-to-school telephones for children who could not attend school because of severe disability. The program was later absorbed by the Special Education Division of the Minnesota Department of Education.

Active committees in Hennepin and Ramsey counties and Duluth aided the Association. Kate (Mrs. Arthur) Barnes, Association founder and second vice-president who was seriously injured in the Cloquet forest fire of 1918, led the Duluth group. She had been treated in California and in Rochester, and she went to Marblehead Sanatorium in Boston for further help. There she was so impressed with the new occupational therapy that she initiated a therapy program in Duluth in 1922. This program led to the formation of the Duluth Crippled Children's Committee, the Duluth Association for the Physically Handicapped (1927), the Kate Barnes classes for crippled children (1927), and much later to the Duluth Rehabilitation Center (1953).

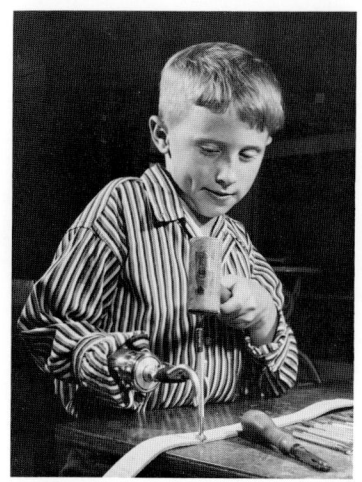

Kenny Patterson works at occupational therapy at Curative Workshop in 1957.

In 1933 the Association, needing continuous funding for its programs, became an affiliate of the National Society for Crippled Children and Adults and adopted Easter Seals as a fund-raising device. That same year, the Association turned to the problem of employment for disabled adults and lobbied successfully for the passage of a bill establishing a loan fund for vocational training. It also voted to present a resolution urging government units to set an example for private industry by employing disabled individuals.

To provide training, employment, and income for homebound men and women, the Association initiated the Lone Craftsman program in 1934. According to an early newsletter:

> On August 1, 1934, Miss Pearl Kenning, a graduate of the Department of Home Economics, University of Minnesota, was employed by the Association to travel throughout the state teaching the "shut-in" cripple to become economically useful. Since August 1, forty-four Lone Craftsmen have received service and we have sold $129.50 worth of products.

The program later became a separate corporation supported by fees from the state, and in 1968 it rejoined its parent organization to become Courage Homecrafters.

In a further effort to locate children in need of help, the Association, with the Minnesota Public Health Association, in 1934 sponsored orthopedic clinics in 30 counties. The Association also operated a direct-aid program on a limited basis, providing braces and limbs and equipment such as wheelchairs and hospital beds as well as transportation to clinics and hospitals.

In 1935 President Franklin D. Roosevelt, disabled from polio, signed legislation dramatically changing the rehabilitation scene and the focus of the Association. The Social Security Act established a new department and funding for three divisions—social welfare, public institutions, and employment and security. Providing old age and survivors' benefits, unemployment compensation, and programs for disabled children and adults, the law was the federal government's first recognition that assistance to disabled persons was a matter of social justice, not charity.

Minnesota set up the Bureau of Services for Crippled Children in 1936 to carry out that law. The bureau was to:

ascertain and employ . . . services for locating crippled children, and for providing medical, surgical, corrective and other services and care facilities for diagnosis, hospitalization and after-care for children who are crippled or who are suffering from conditions that lead to crippling.

With those needs met by state and national programs, the Association refocused attention on others, such as lending equipment to people who did not qualify for other resources. The Association also contributed toward the cost of artificial limbs, hearing aids, and braces supplied by Social Security, which required matching funds that Minnesota did not provide.

Louis Lehman, below in 1938, helped support his family by making metalware objects for the Lone Craftsman program.

3 Camping: An Experiment

With growing awareness of the importance of new treatment programs like the physical therapy department at Mayo Clinic, the world of disabilities was changing. In 1936, the Association became the Minnesota Association for Crippled Children and Disabled Adults. Two years later, board member Jennie Dowling took up the cause of camping for disabled children and adults.

Johanna "Jennie" Bordewich, born in 1872 in Minnesota Falls, is believed to have been the first white child born in Yellow Medicine County. She grew up in Granite Falls, where she became acquainted with her father's friend, Michael J. Dowling. They were married on October 2, 1895, and had three daughters—Marjorie, Kathleen, and Dorothy. During World War I, Jennie Dowling was active in relief work, serving as charter member of the Olivia and Renville County Red Cross and on the Renville child welfare board. She was postmistress in Olivia and a social service worker for the Veterans Bureau, and she served on the Governor's Relief Committee in 1932. Later she worked as a proofreader in the secretary of state's office and in a clerical position for the Department of Social Security in St. Paul.

In her work and travels, Jennie Dowling had seen firsthand the problems that could beset disabled individuals. Many unable to attend school or work faced grim futures. What could the Association do to make their lives more meaningful? A few states, she knew, had experimented with camping programs for people with disabilities. She decided to commit her time and energies to making that experience possible in Minnesota.

In 1938 Jennie Dowling almost single-handedly organized an experimental 10-day camping session at St. John's Landing Camp, in what was then known as the St. Croix National Recreation Area, east of Hinckley. She had no guidelines. Calling on friends for help with transportation and funds, she launched an activity that would become a major part of the organization's work. Jennie and Michael Dowling's daughter Kathleen B. Dowling of St. Paul recalled in 1988:

> Our mother started the camp and had us opening envelopes with dollar bills in them to pay for buses, food, and so forth. We would sit around the dining room table and count money and make lists. [The people who helped] were all volunteers, including Mother, my cousin Marie Geer and her husband Arthur from Minneapolis, Carolyn Conroy who drove and helped Marie mail out letters asking for money, and Marie's brother, Harald Bordewich, who worked at the Hinckley camp.

The dollars provided camp activities such as nature hikes, crafts, swimming, boating, singing, dramatics, picnicking, archery, croquet, indoor games, evening programs, Sunday services, and the camp newspaper, *The Pine Trees Whisper*.

Jennie Dowling

The experiment demonstrated that camping was indeed feasible for people with disabilities and that it provided them valuable social and recreational experiences. A second session was held in 1939, but available funds did not stretch far enough for a session in 1940. In 1941, while serving her second year as volunteer Association board president and executive secretary, Dowling organized an eight-week session at Head of the Rapids Camp on the St. Croix River, then part of the St. Croix Recreation Area. The camp had been built by the Civilian Conservation Corps and veterans of World War I. A total of 160 campers attended that year, with expenditures of $4,192.11.

Jennie Dowling took a leave of absence from the Division of Crippled Children to run both the summer program and, in her spare time, the affairs of the Association. She hired young Toivo "Toy" Jambeck to direct the 1941-42 sessions. Swimming coach at Roosevelt High School in Minneapolis, Jambeck took time out from 1943 to 1946 for World War II service. During his absence, the camp took on a Western theme and was called Dowling Cowboy Ranch, in honor of Jennie Dowling. Jambeck returned in 1946 to serve as camping director until 1960.

Elmer Josephs of Richfield worked as a counselor at Head of the Rapids Camp when he was 19. All the counselors then were disabled, and Josephs wore a leg brace because of a disability. He said:

> It was my first opportunity to work in a situation with my handicapped peers, and the experience helped me mature and build my belief in my own abilities. Camp was important to counselors and campers alike. It helped them determine their own futures and live their own lives. Camp was the first step.

Josephs later helped organize the Service Club for the Handicapped, served as its president, and helped develop several national organizations working for people with disabilities. He also supported efforts to remove environmental barriers from the community, while enjoying a career as a pharmacist.

In 1946 camp sessions moved to Camp Kiwanis, a site near Marine on St. Croix, leased from the St. Paul Kiwanis Club for a dollar a year. A 1947 brochure designated sessions for "children with speech problems, orthopedically crippled children outside the Twin Cities, disabled adults, children with cardiac difficulties, Twin Cities crippled children, and wheelchair cases." The inclusion of children with speech and hearing impairments in the Kiwanis program grew

Dick and Helen Olson

RICHARD R. OLSON: 47 YEARS AT CAMP

Dick Olson, affectionately known as Uncle Al to thousands of campers, has been part of Courage Center's camping program almost since its birth:

I heard about the first camp in 1938 at Marshall University High School. Mrs. Dowling ran the camp that year. She mended the camp sheets and blankets at her home during the winter and bought all the food herself. I attended camp from 1941 to 1946, when I joined the staff as a counselor at Kiwanis, and I've worked at Courage camps ever since—as tour guide, general assistant, and friend to campers. I've made wonderful friends. In fact, I met my future wife, Helen Torgelson, at Kiwanis in 1947—we were married outdoors at Camp Courage in 1973. One of the fun camp traditions has been my birthday party, held every session. We have cake, candles, everything. I figure that after 47 years at camp, I must be at least 200 years old!

Campers arrive at Camp Kiwanis in the early 1940s.

Young people enjoy the scenic beauty and rustic environment of Camp Kiwanis, in the 1940s.

Camp Kiwanis campers had to be transported to nearby Square Lake for swimming.

out of a 1946 mobile speech clinic sponsored by the Association and the University of Minnesota to discover speech and hearing problems in 22 Minnesota counties. The clinic operated for several years, testing more than 75,000 children.

Marvin Thompson of St. Cloud recalled in 1988 that his Kiwanis experience was "a beautiful transition to living on my own." In a wheelchair because of polio, he reveled in being away from home, making friends, and learning to love the outdoors:

> I went on to Macalester College in St. Paul and lived in a dorm. I hired someone to help and experienced the same freedom I had felt at camp. I got a doctorate in English and a master's degree in music at the University of Minnesota and taught Shakespeare at St. Cloud State, retiring in 1980.

Camp Kiwanis was a beautiful site far above the St. Croix River, but it was small and inadequate for campers with disabilities. Campers had to be carried down many steps for canoeing in the river and transported five miles to a beach at Square Lake for swimming. The eight cottages, each housing eight campers, lacked water and heat. The need for a new camping facility was obvious.

4 A New Name and a New Focus: Rehabilitation

Citizens' efforts directed toward winning World War II and building a society at peace made for a difficult period for the Association, and the sketchy records of the 1940s and early 1950s indicate frequent changes in leadership. Nevertheless, executive directors including Jean C. Pierce, C. Lindquist, Robert Booth, and Harold R. Gabrielson, led the organization in providing limited services in three areas: direct-aid equipment, a mobile hearing clinic, and summer camping.

The 1940s also saw far-reaching legislation affecting both the people with disabilities and the organizations serving them. In 1943 the Barden-LaFollette Act provided for vocational training for veterans and civilians and established the Office of Vocational Rehabilitation. The return of 670,800 wounded American veterans from World War II necessitated both new facilities and programs.

Rehabilitation facilities were needed to respond to a growing epidemic of poliomyelitis as well. The Sister Elizabeth Kenny Institute opened in Minneapolis in 1942 to serve polio patients, and Sheltering Arms, built in Minneapolis as an orphanage in 1882, served as a hospital for polio patients from 1942 to 1955, when Jonas Salk's vaccine dramatically halted the epidemic. In 1945, the University of Minnesota received a grant leading to the development of an extensive rehabilitation program under the direction of Frederic J. Kottke, a physician at the University of Minnesota Hospitals.

Still associated with the National Society for Crippled Children and Adults, the Association changed its name in 1947 to the Minnesota Society for Crippled Children and Adults, Inc. Frank Krusen, physician at Mayo Clinic, chairman of the American Medical Association Council on Physical Medicine and Rehabilitation, and Society board member, added his endorsement to the increasing demand for rehabilitation facilities. The Society responded to growing interest in rehabilitation by directing its efforts toward the establishment of a network of rehabilitation centers. Board president Frank M. Rarig Jr., executive secretary of the Amherst H. Wilder Charity in St. Paul, led the organization along its new course, designed to make rehabilitation services available all over the state.

The first Society-sponsored facility was the St. Paul Rehabilitation Center, established in 1948 in the remodeled Wilder public baths at 319 Eagle Street, in cooperation with the St. Paul Junior League and the Wilder Charity. According to the Society's newsletter, the new facility would "straighten limbs, train muscles and reduce handicaps" for individuals from 4 months to 91 years of age. The former Wilder public bath and swimming pool would house "polio patients learning to walk again, veterans learning how to use artificial limbs, and cerebral palsy victims learning to help themselves."

Frank Rarig Jr.

The center, like those to follow, offered occupational and physical therapy, social services, vocational counseling, and other activities designed to carry out rehabilitation, defined by Dr. Krusen as "a restoration through personal health services of handicapped individuals to the fullest physical, mental, social, and economic usefulness of which they are capable."

Continuing a joint effort, the Society and the Minneapolis Junior League established a children's cerebral palsy preschool in the Minneapolis Curative Workshop in 1949. Working with the Duluth Junior League and other local supporters in 1951, the Society established the Duluth Rehabilitation Center. The structure of the first two centers set the pattern. They were locally incorporated with separate boards of directors, affiliated with the Society for financial help and administrative guidance. As they became more sophisticated and achieved a higher level of local support, they became independent.

In 1978, Frank Rarig described the status of the Minnesota Society for Crippled Children and Adults in the early 1950s:

> The Society was a struggling organization. Two of its major problems were gaining public recognition and making people aware of its needs. Our only source of funds in the 1940s was the annual crippled children's mail appeal, and as more and more charities got into the direct mail fund-raising business, the average donation to the Society went down and our fund-raising expenses went up. When we were looking for a director, Wilko Schoenbohm was recommended . . . it was one of the best things that ever happened to us.

Wilko B. Schoenbohm was hired as executive director of the Society in 1952, following a ten-year tenure as superintendent of the Crippled Children's School (now the Anne Carlsen School) in Jamestown, North Dakota, and four years as the first director of the Iowa Hospital School for severely handicapped children, in Iowa City. Modeled after the Jamestown facility, the hospital school became a training center for people working in rehabilitation. Schoenbohm helped plan and develop both facilities.

A native of Denver, Iowa, and the son of a Lutheran minister, Schoenbohm had earned a bachelor's degree at Wartburg College in Waverly, Iowa, and a master's degree from the State University of Iowa. He did graduate work at Wartburg Seminary in Dubuque, Iowa, and at Wayne University in Detroit, and he studied for two years at European universities and centers, including a renowned center for handicapped people in Bethel, Germany. He was greatly influenced by the center's director, Dr. Friedrich Von Bodelschwingh, who emphasized that "The secret of ministering is the ability to listen. The person who fails to listen is not competent to lead."

Wilko B. Schoenbohm in 1952

One of the first acts of the new executive director of the Minnesota Society for Crippled Children and Adults was to establish a development committee to define organizational goals. The development and future planning committee recommended that the Society focus on four major areas: education and legislation, rehabilitation, employment, and camping.

The Society board recognized that to effect changes benefiting disabled people, an educated public and continuing support of legislation would be necessary. In the early 1950s staff members spoke to groups throughout Minnesota, built up a film collection and publication library, and cosponsored an institute on the education of disabled children.

In 1953, Schoenbohm helped organize and was the first president of the Minnesota Council for Special Education, a group that campaigned successfully for a legislative interim commission to study problems of handicapped children in the state. A short time later the board established a development fund into which all unrestricted bequests were placed to finance growth. Fund-raising efforts expanded to include not only the mail campaign but also special events such as style shows. Membership drives, coin cards, memorial gifts, and increased solicitation from individuals and businesses broadened the Society's efforts and resulted in greater income.

The Society continued its support of the network of rehabilitation centers while turning its attention to the need for sheltered employment for individuals whose disabilities kept them out of the marketplace. In the early 1950s, the Society employed 10 disabled individuals to work on mailings and other piecework projects in a pilot program at its headquarters at 1639 Hennepin Avenue in Minneapolis. Needing space to expand its workshop and other

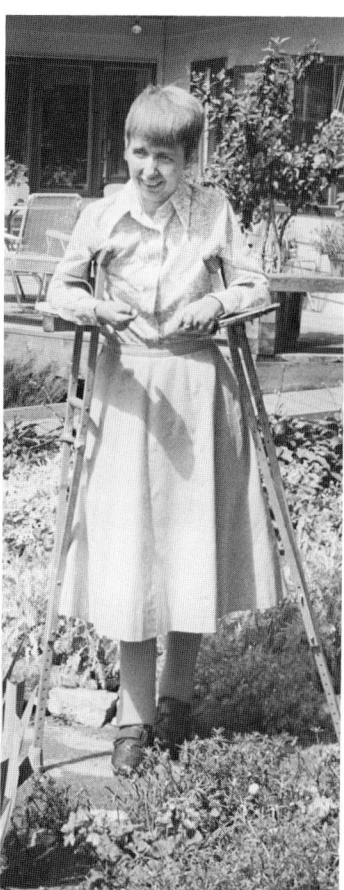

JOYCE VINCENT: MAKING THE WORLD A BETTER PLACE

I got arthritis very severely when I was 11. It was devastating—everything was painful and within two years no joints would move. I was in Shriners Hospital 13 months in 1946 and 1947. There doctors forced my legs straight under anesthesia and put them in casts. I could walk slowly with one or two-inch steps.

I started working for the Society in July 1955, as a receptionist, for $80 a month. I also helped with equipment loan records, bookkeeping, and record-keeping of income by county. Later I moved into other jobs including accounting, writing for the newsletter, and handling printing. I became office coordinator in 1970 and coordinated the move to Courage Center in 1973. About 65 or 70 people moved in, 35 or so from 2004 Lyndale and the rest from Curative Workshop and Homecrafters.

Through the years, Courage Center has encouraged my development. That's what's so special about this place. I had some basic abilities and was blessed with parents with a can-do attitude. Courage Center gave me the opportunity to grow. I now direct the Courage Cards program, a big project with about two million cards sold annually.

Courage Center staff also helped me with ideas for an accessible home. I always had the dream of having my own house. With the goal of living independently, I went through seven surgical replacements: hips, knees, ankles, elbow, and some jaw surgery. I worked for five years, with daily therapy, weight lifting, and stretching to strengthen my legs enough to stand and walk on my own. When surgery had done what it could to improve my range of motion, I started looking for a house. Real estate agents carried me up lots of steps! Then in 1981 I was reading a book on solar homes, and I said, "Joyce, you're going to design and build your own solar home. It's going to happen." In August 1982, I moved into my own home, an energy-efficient, accessible house in northeast Minneapolis.

I try to stay active in the community. I've served on the board of directors of the Minneapolis YWCA and the Minneapolis Zonta Club, and I work to support issues for women, environment, and peace. I'm also a volunteer with the Minneapolis Literacy Program, and I was a delegate to the 1980 Democratic National Convention in New York City. I went on to Washington, D.C., and visited the White House at President Jimmy Carter's invitation. Recently I received the first City of Minneapolis award for outstanding citizens who have worked to make Minneapolis a better community.

People ask what motivates me. First, I believe in making the world a better place to live, within the scope of my reach. I can't change the world, but if I can do something where I am, that is part of my purpose.

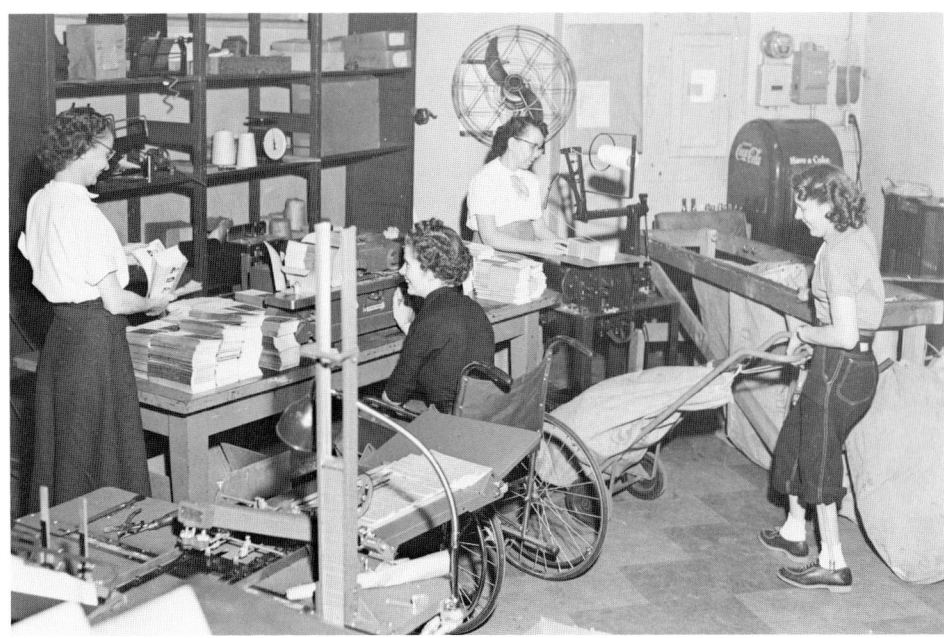
Employees work on mailing and piecework projects, in the early 1950s.

programs, the Society moved to a former warehouse at 420 East Lake Street in 1956. There it piloted a program for subcontract work including the assembly of dolls. When the project proved economically unfeasible, it was discontinued.

The list of rehabilitation centers and workshops launched with the Society's help is impressive:
- St. Paul Rehabilitation Center (1948)
- Duluth Rehabilitation Center (1951, new facility named Nat G. Polinsky Rehabilitation Center in 1967)
- Mankato Rehabilitation Center (1953, new facility in 1965)
- Iron Range Rehabilitation Center, Virginia (1954)
- Winona Rehabilitation Center (1955)
- Ability Building Center, Rochester (1957, expanded in 1965)
- Western Minnesota Rehabilitation and Referral Agency, Montevideo (1958)
- Minneapolis Rehabilitation Center (1960)
- St. Cloud Opportunity Training Center (1962)
- Cedar Valley Rehabilitation Center, Austin (1963)
- West Central Industries, Willmar (1967)
- Lake Region Sheltered Workshop, Fergus Falls (1967)

Except for the Winona Rehabilitation Center, which merged with the local hospital shortly after it was established, the centers experienced significant growth and became independent organizations.

The Ability Building Center (ABC, Inc.) in Rochester is an example of how one sheltered workshop came to be. In the mid-1950s Carl Bauman, an elderly bachelor from Pine Island, read about Camp Courage in the newspaper. He contacted the Society and offered to donate some land and a large, old home in Pine Island for a camp for people with disabilities.

Employees at ABC Workshop in Rochester in 1988

Society board members Elizabeth (Mrs. George) Lowry and Dr. Frank Krusen of Rochester and Wilko Schoenbohm met with Bauman. They told him that while they appreciated his offer, the property was not appropriate for a camping facility. They suggested that the Society sell the property and use the proceeds to establish a sheltered workshop facility in Rochester, where there was more need as well as more support services.

Bauman agreed and donated the property to the Society in 1956. The Society sold it for $6,000, using the funds to establish the Ability Building Center in 1957. That year ABC had three employees working on subcontract jobs, including the assembly of 50,000 souvenir drums. Today, it has an annual budget of about $3 million and helps more than 400 clients each year through evaluation, training, and employment at its Rochester facility and at Woodland Industries, a satellite workshop in Caledonia, established in 1980.

IRENE LOHMANN: THE KEY IS ENCOURAGEMENT

When Irene "Willie" Lohmann left Zumbrota and moved to Minneapolis to find work, she didn't realize her first job would turn into a lifetime commitment. She started working for the Minnesota Society for Crippled Children and Adults in 1955 in the mailroom, making addressograph plates. Cerebral palsy had affected Lohmann's right side, so she used just one hand to operate the platemaker, later a typewriter, and then a computer. She took on more and more responsibility, handling equipment loan, clerical duties, and secretarial jobs in public relations and rehabilitation areas. Now she is program assistant for the Courage Stroke Network.

The year 1975 was Lohmann's "most exciting." She received the National Association of Rehabilitation Secretaries Service Award, in recognition of her dedication, hard work, and talent. "Courage Center has been a big part of my life," she said. "I've set goals and people have encouraged me. I have really enjoyed every area I've worked in. The key is encouragement."

Camper Brian Altman hitches a ride from a counselor at Camp Courage in 1958. Altman worked on the camp staff from 1971 to 1976 and later became a media specialist at the Michael Dowling Urban Environmental Learning Center (formerly Michael Dowling School).

5 Camp Courage

Despite its inadequate facilities, Camp Kiwanis had opened up a world of outdoor adventures to children and adults with disabilities. The Society was determined to expand these efforts and made building a new camp top priority in 1953. Wilko Schoenbohm explained:

> We realized that camping can positively influence individuals' attitudes toward themselves. The way they view their own disabilities is often more crucial than the disability itself. By breaking out of isolation to share with others the fun of camping in a natural setting, they can see themselves more objectively.

Nobel Shadduck of Annandale chaired the camping committee, which began planning the new camp and searching for a site. Other members were Gretchen (Mrs. Hugo, Jr.) Schlenk of Cloquet, Frank Rarig and Raymond J. Wachtler, D.D.S., of St. Paul, and H. G. Metcalf of Fairmont. Harry B. Gough of St. Cloud was president of the board, and Shadduck told him, "You'd better not make me chairman of that committee. It might wind up near Annandale." The committee examined many sites, hoping to find one on a lake within 50 miles of the Twin Cities. And it turned down a couple of offers for free but inadequate land.

Shadduck did find a beautiful 40-acre wooded site with a 3,800-foot shoreline on Cedar Lake in Wright County, between Annandale and Maple Lake. The owner agreed to sell it for $8,500—almost all the money in the Society's development fund. Schoenbohm then turned to Thomas Ellerbe, owner of Ellerbe Architects, for help in designing the camp. Ellerbe had given the campers at Camp Kiwanis rides in his boat on the St. Croix River, and he was interested in the work of the Society.

Ellerbe agreed to plan the camp with payment at a later date, assigning architect Larry Hovick to the job. Agreeing with the committee on the therapeutic value of a beautiful environment, Hovick designed the camp to be unique, to have height and vision instead of just a rustic look. William Dobson, from a Minneapolis advertising firm, suggested the name Camp Courageous. Shortened to Camp Courage, the name caught the imagination of the planners, who immediately adopted it.

With design for Camp Courage underway, the Society turned to finding money to pay for it. Chairman E. K. "Bud" Thorgaard of Minneapolis headed the fund-raising committee, and volunteers and staff began contacting friends and potential donors to the capital campaign. The goal of $147,000 included:
- $5,000 each for eight double cabins
- $25,000 for the dining hall/recreation center
- $10,000 for a therapy and health center

- $10,000 for an art, craft, and hobby shop
- $5,000 for a nature study lodge
- $2,500 for an outdoor chapel

Staff members traveled around the state speaking to clubs and organizations on behalf of Camp Courage and presenting specific projects for support. Schoenbohm stressed the importance of this work:

> Many people feel programs for handicapped individuals are more important than the fund-raising aspect—raising money seems like a mundane task. But if there's no money, all your beautiful ideas don't accomplish much. Fund-raising done honestly and conscientiously is just as much God's work as programming.

Camp Courage cabins

Others agreed, and as organizations, corporations, and individuals responded favorably to the appeal, the Camp Courage fund grew. The Minnesota Association of Moose Lodges sponsored the first cabin, and other organizations and donors followed suit. By March 1954, the fund had reached $60,000, and in July the Society broke ground for the camp. Glenn Cunningham, a national track star who had overcome disabilities caused by severe burns, spoke at the groundbreaking.

By late winter 1954, six cabins and the dining hall/recreation center were underway. But with funds running out, it looked like the building program would have to come to a halt. Les Park, of the Baker Foundation in Minneapolis, then informed the Society of a $15,000 grant, enabling construction to continue and the camp to open.

By the time camp opened for a limited session in June 1955, completed buildings included six cabins housing 16 campers and 4 counselors each, the dining hall/recreation center, a therapy building, and craftshop. About 300 campers aged 8 to 19 attended the first session, marveling at the accessibility of the buildings and grounds and moving through their daily adventures with a sense of independence. For the first time in Minnesota, children with physical limitations could explore nature, try new activities, enjoy friendships, and benefit from therapy in an accessible camp built especially for them.

Participating in the July 7, 1954, groundbreaking for Camp Courage are (left to right) Nobel Shadduck, president of the board of the Society; Glenn Cunningham, world-famous track star; Karen Stokes, 1954 poster girl; and Governor C. Elmer Anderson.

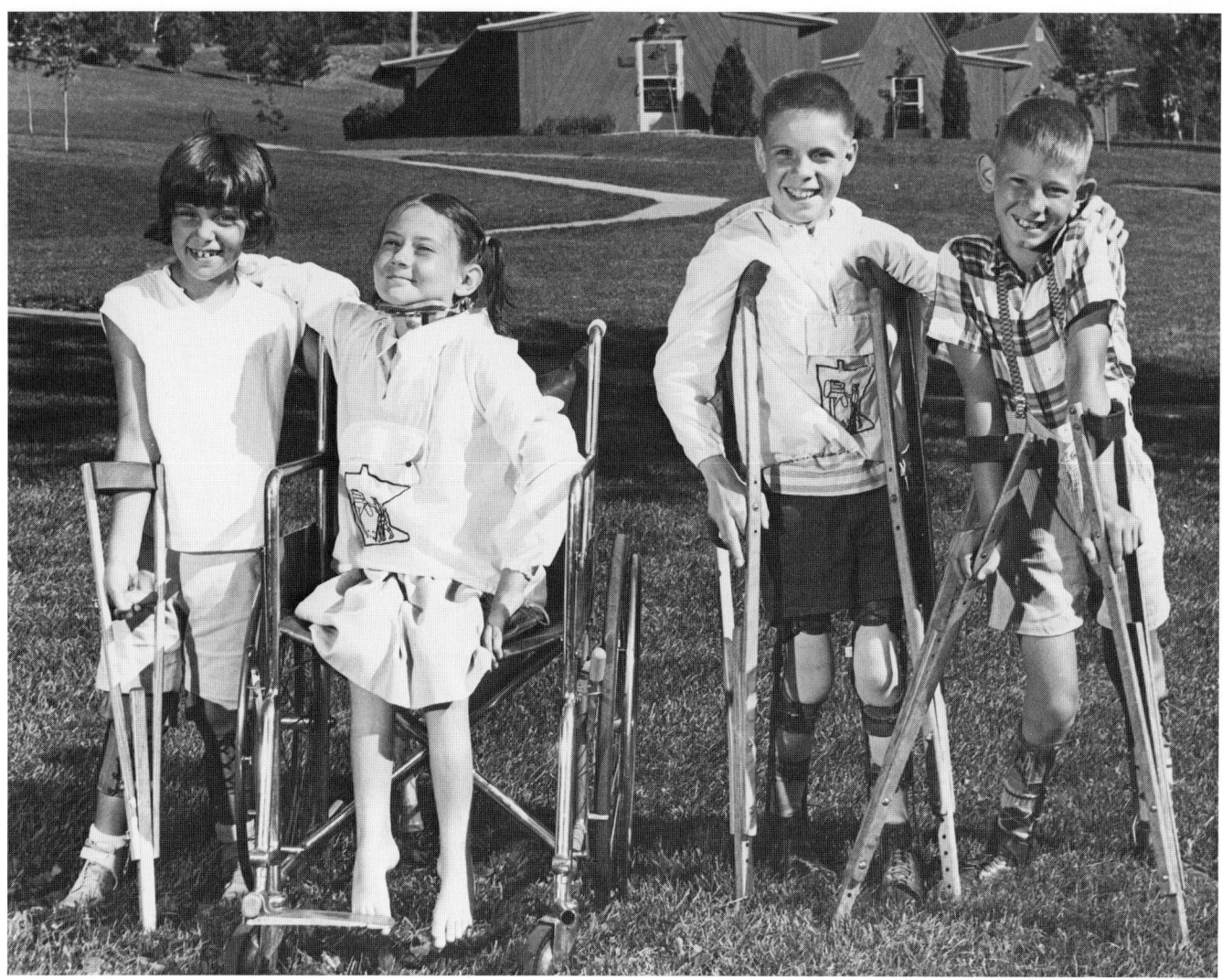

These campers include Camp Courage Children of the Year Debby McGrane of St. Paul and Harold Kiewel of Jordan (center, 1964) and Marian Charles of St. Paul and Francis Walther of Avoka (1965).

JUDY VOSS: IT ALL WORKED OUT FINE

Jack and Judy Voss worked at Camp Courage and later at Courage North, where Jack was director until his death in 1980. Judy served as director from 1980 to 1987:

I was at Camp Courage the first year it opened and there when it expanded later to include the speech camp and added the pool, gym, and reception center. My husband, Jack, and I called our Courage experiences the best part of our lives. Jack was a teacher and swim coach at Minneapolis Vocational High School. He met Toy Jambeck at a swim meet, and Toy asked him to work at the camp as waterfront director. I became the first nurse.

    The summer the camp opened was exciting, with everything shiny and new. There was no extra housing, and it wasn't until we got to camp that we found out Jack would be sleeping in a camper cabin and the two children and I would be in "the penthouse" [over the dining hall] with the two cooks and the kitchen girls. And where was the health center? There were two large bathrooms on the main floor of the dining hall, and one of those became the infirmary. There was room for a cot, a table, and a makeshift bookcase with medical supplies. There was no camp doctor then. When a camper was ill enough to see a doctor, we drove to Maple Lake to visit Dr. Raetz. Amazingly, it all worked out just fine.

An autographed photo of Joe Foss and his daughter, Cheryl, in 1956

The first campers represented a variety of disabilities, resulting primarily from polio and cerebral palsy, but also from muscular dystrophy, rheumatoid arthritis, blindness, accident injuries, congenital deformities, and head injuries. Speech therapy was provided to campers needing it.

Donors had responded generously to the fund drive for building Camp Courage, but operating funds were also needed. The new camp program tripled the camping budget with additional staff, more campers in need of financial assistance, and other expenses, so the Society launched an active fund-raising program to cover growing costs. "Send a crippled child to camp" became the theme, and the Society soon adopted a plan asking donors to donate "camperships" at $50 for a two-week session for one child at camp. Again, people in the community gave generously.

In 1956 a nature building and a chapel-amphitheater were added to the campsite. South Dakota governor Joe Foss and disabled Metropolitan Opera star Marjorie Lawrence helped dedicate Camp Courage on July 8 that year. Wilko Schoenbohm remembered:

> We had invited Joe Foss to participate in the dedication of Camp Courage. His daughter, who had cerebral palsy, had been in the Jamestown School when I was there. He said, "I don't know if I can get away—I'll let you know." Sunday morning, the day of the dedication, the phone rang: "I'm coming. You got an alfalfy patch I can set down on? You just get the Maple Lake firemen out there to wave me down." Sure enough, just before the program began, a little plane landed with Joe at the controls and his daughter Cheryl alongside. When I asked Cheryl how the trip was, she said, "Rough as a cob!"

More additions to the camp followed: cottages for the caretaker, resident doctor, and camp director, given by Minnie Hull of St. Paul; a fragrance garden established and maintained by the Lake Minnetonka Garden Club; a trailside garden funded by board member Harold Tearse in memory of his mother, Kate Horton Tearse; the Boutell self-guiding nature trail; and a small animal zoo, given by the Lions clubs.

What set the camp apart from others in the nation was its willingness to take in severely disabled and high-risk campers and its flexibility in adding new disability groups as they emerged. While recreation was a primary goal, therapy was also important: To make camping a worthwhile experience, children with disabilities had to participate, had to be continually challenged, had to have opportunities to learn new things to help fill and motivate their lives during the 353 days a year when they were not at camp.

From the day it opened, Camp Courage received national recognition for its innovative design and programming, and no one appreciated it more than the campers. A letter to the *Minneapolis Tribune* in 1961 revealed:

> The campers were all handicapped. Some had to be fed every meal, some lifted in and out of bed by hydraulic lifters. More wore heavy braces, used crutches, or carried canes. Some had speech difficulties so serious it was impossible for them to communicate. These brave people must have suffered untold agonies of pain and heartache for many years, and yet the spirit they displayed at camp was something to see. They played tricks on each other, laughed out loud, sang songs, told funny stories, played games, and went fishing. There was not a tear or an irritable word, and many of them lived in a different world the entire week.

Campers enjoy the fragrance garden at Camp Courage, in 1985

These people earned extra stars for their heavenly crowns by their unselfish attitude and genuine interest in each other. I thought I had seen courage before, but I didn't even know the meaning of the word. Camp Courage—what else could they call it? . . . I know. I was a camper.—HELEN E. BOYCE, MINNEAPOLIS

With the facilities complete, the Society turned its attention to a group with special needs. In addition to attending Camp Courage, some campers with speech, hearing, and language impairments attended special sessions at Camp Kiwanis for several years after the new camp opened. It was clear that these children had different needs and interests from campers with physical disabilities. In 1963 the Society purchased 30 wooded acres adjacent to Camp Courage and began raising funds to build a separate campus for them.

Counselor Mary Martin of Sartell, Minnesota, helps camper Lori Eavis from Michigan improve her speech, in 1981.

Edmund C. Meierbachtol of Le Sueur spearheaded the fund-raising effort. The community of donors responded again, and construction began in August 1964 to be completed in time for the 1966 summer session. The new buildings, dedicated on August 14, 1966, included a dining hall/recreation center, a speech therapy center built by the Minnesota Future Farmers of America, and six cabins built by clubs and individuals. New facilities shared by the units were a reception center sponsored by the Veterans of Foreign Wars and an indoor swimming pool made possible by a gift from Mary and Harold W. Sweatt of Wayzata, in memory of their son William R. Sweatt Jr., who died of polio.

Hubert H. Humphrey, vice-president of the United States, spoke at the 1966 dedication of the speech and hearing unit of Camp Courage. In a moving tribute, he said:

> This camp is a living prayer—because it does what religion asks us to do. A minister in our home church preached a sermon in which he said, "The way you treat people is the way you treat God." I have thought of that message every day since . . . to me this camp indicates that a lot of people are treating God pretty good.

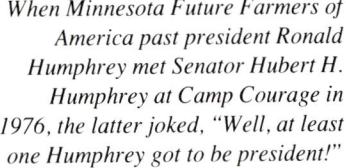

When Minnesota Future Farmers of America past president Ronald Humphrey met Senator Hubert H. Humphrey at Camp Courage in 1976, the latter joked, "Well, at least one Humphrey got to be president!"

Overnights on Humphrey Island are a highlight for campers at a 1962 session including (left to right) Konnie Christ of Minneapolis, Beverly Knorr of Hutchinson, Barbara Nemmers of Appleton, and Deborah Klitzke of Litchfield.

    Construction of the Judith Ann King Recreation Center (with a gym and stage) funded by Clarence and Lucile King of St. Paul, in memory of their daughter, followed in 1970. A Rotary activities building available to both units, a Lions craft and nature building, and a greenhouse built by the Minnesota Future Farmers of America were also added. In 1974, a fire destroyed the reception center, wiping out the library of books, periodicals, records and films, and the nature museum and its collection of wildflower paintings, butterflies and moths, and Indian artifacts. In 1975 an enlarged, improved, fire-resistant building was built on the same location with the same design.

    The Camp Courage site grew along with its facilities, adding an adjoining farm and another 17-acre island on Lake Koronis. That island was named Winther Island after its donors, Dr. and Mrs. C. P. Winther of Paynesville. By 1965 Camp Courage had grown to 191 acres, and by 1983 to 305.

Hubert and Muriel Humphrey were longtime friends of Camp Courage. In 1955 they had donated $283 won on the television game show "Masquerade Party" to the camp. They dressed as Minnehaha and Hiawatha and stumped the panel trying to guess their identities. Humphrey did it again in 1958, dressed as a University of Minnesota football player, donating $500 to the camp.

In 1959 Humphrey helped to acquire a 17-acre island adjacent to Camp Courage from the Department of the Interior. Funds donated by the Humphreys were used to buy the property, originally known as Mink Island, later named Humphrey Island. The island was developed into an overnight camping and nature study site, as described by Melvin P. Vollhaber, St. Paul, longtime board member, volunteer, and member of the Minnesota Moose Association:

> The Moose Association gave the Society $10,000 to develop the island. Volunteers came from many different chapters, and we hauled lumber over on an old pontoon boat in the summer and by truck on the ice in the winter. We worked on weekends, and my wife said, "There must be something to this program you're involved in—you've missed two summers of golf!"
>
> Well, we built the shelter using hand tools and makeshift hoists. Then we had to build a cement floor. I went to Buffalo and said to the cement man, "I need some cement for Camp Courage for the island project." And he agreed, so I said, "Follow me." So we drive and drive and drive, and stop in a farmer's yard and look at the shore of the island, and he says,"Where is it going?" And I point to the island and say, "Over there." Then he said to me, "You must be insane." You see, there was a sandbar, and we knew he could drive on it to the island— we had been driving it with an old army duck. We put stakes along the sandbar to show him where to drive and he said, "Well, okay. I'm just as crazy as you." So he got the cement over there and drove the truck back. I say, "Thanks a lot, pal." He looks at me and says, "Don't call me. I'll call you."
>
> It has been a great experience, being involved with Camp Courage. We all had such faith that it would work out, and it did. The early clubs provided the motivation for others to follow.

Carl M. Halker: A family affair

Carl Halker signed on in 1966 to help with a Camp Courage pilot program for children with speech and hearing impairments, and he has been clinical director of the program ever since. A speech and language pathologist with the Edina public schools, Halker directs a staff of professional speech and language clinicians from school districts throughout the nation.

Camp is a family affair for Carl and Marilyn Halker. Their son, Nils 24, who was 15 months old when speech camp opened in 1966, worked as waterfront director for several summers. Their oldest daughter, Heidi 21, is a unit leader, and Kari 19 joined the staff as a counselor for the 1989 season. "Our whole family has spent every summer at Camp Courage for the past 24 years," Carl said.

Camp Courage is a way of life for the Halker family: Carl, director of the speech and hearing program (right), Nils (standing), Heidi (center), and Kari (left).

6 Removing Barriers and Gaining Independence

From the successful Camp Courage experience grew a new awareness of the pressing need to provide activities and involvement for people with disabilities on a year-round basis. The Society recognized two major areas of need to reach that goal: a comprehensive residential rehabilitation center and an aggressive program to break down barriers—physical and attitudinal—that blocked full participation in the community. The Society turned first to the problem of architectural barriers.

The idea of changing the environment to enable individuals to participate in society was a long time coming. For years, the public's attitude had been that disabled people should be cared for somewhere out of view. Now more people were aware that people with disabilities could function in the community—if the community were more accessible. Rehabilitation centers and workshops were helping people throughout the state and the nation. But what good was retraining and rehabilitation if the individual could not get into the workplace?

In 1958 the Society formed one of the first architectural barriers committees in the nation to study and make recommendations about the problem of inaccessibility. Henry Haverstock Jr., a Minneapolis attorney and early polio patient of Sister Kenny, was named chairman. He wrote for the Society newsletter:

> It is simply amazing how many libraries, post offices, court houses, churches, and other public buildings are still being built with a long line of stairs leading up to them . . . with no thought being given to the fact that it prevents a large segment of our disabled people from using them. This is a form of discrimination which our committee intends to militate against, so all of our citizens are given easy access to public places.

Looking back in 1988, Haverstock summed up the project's achievements:

> The committee was a moving force in obtaining local legislation mandating the installation of curb cuts at intersections, facilitating wheelchair access, bringing about the codification and adoption of one of the first state laws mandating the modification of public buildings to facilitate handicapped access, and in preparing standards for construction of nongovernmental buildings.
>
> These standards, which apply both to new buildings and to major renovations of existing buildings, are now mandated by law. They are comprehensive and apply to such things as door widths, toilet access for wheelchairs, elevators, elevation standards as to ramps, and many more.
>
> The committee was instrumental in securing passage of federal legislation mandating wheelchair access into and within all federal buildings. Courage Center also was prime mover in the development of the handicapped access symbol and special parking spaces for disabled individuals.

Henry Haverstock in 1958

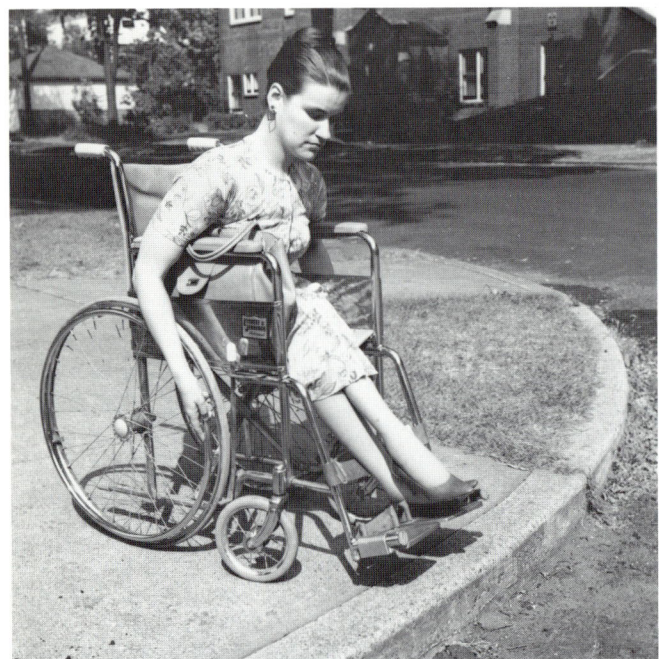
Society staff member Leslee Coffield of Minneapolis demonstrates the need for curb cuts, in the 1960s.

Inaccessible phone booths were barriers in the 1960s.

The Society received a two-year grant in 1961 from the U.S. Office of Vocational Rehabilitation for the nation's first survey of architectural barriers, a grant renewed several times. The committee and staff project director Robert Schwanke surveyed barriers, made recommendations, and legislated for change. Staff member William B. Hopkins took over from Schwanke in 1968 and guided the program through further legislation and development. Hopkins said in 1988:

> In addition to the accomplishments noted by Henry Haverstock, we produced a film, *Sound the Trumpets,* that was shown all over the world. We were also instrumental in the establishment of the State Council for the Handicapped, [now the State Council on Disability], the development of the Department of Human Services' standards for disabled persons, and the standards for specialized transportation vehicles. And we were later the prime mover in the birth and nurturing of Metro Mobility, a public transportation system now providing about 100,000 rides per month to disabled people. We also spearheaded making polling places accessible, now mandated by law.

The Society also helped plan the construction of Southwest State University in Marshall, the first four-year college in the nation built without barriers. Founded by the state legislature in 1963, the college opened in 1967. About 15 percent of its students are physically disabled. Its first president, Howard Bellows, was a Courage Center board member and a strong advocate of barrier-free planning.

While working to make the environment more accessible during the 1960s, the Society did not neglect the growing urgency for a residential center and received many letters and calls from severely disabled young adults urging its early construction. One such letter came from Bob Russ, Blue Earth, who was disabled from cerebral palsy and had attended Camp Courage for many years:

Society headquarters at 2004 Lyndale Avenue South, Minneapolis

The camp was only a partial answer—the two-week periods of living in a functioning society only served to underscore the unmet needs of the severely handicapped who gathered there. Of the hundreds who came from all parts of the state, only a few were able to live and work in the world of "normals." Thus, Camp Courage is a completion and a beginning. Courage is the ultimate in camping facilities; Courage is a bare beginning in the direction of setting up a special facility that would permit the severely handicapped to live in a society of equals.

As things stand, many of these people exist in "terminal nursing homes." They are separated from those around them by as much as 50 years, and by the differences in interests that separate the living from those who are waiting only for death . . . It is not surprising that these people show a steady erosion of their minds and strength that far exceeds the toll demanded by time. What can we do about it? A little—and a lot. No one of us can solve the problem single-handedly, but if we join our voices in a chorus we will be heard in the highest circles.

And what do we ask? A place to live, not a place to die—a dwelling place where we may develop and use those abilities and skills that are within us, where we may live as completely as possible. Is this asking too much? I believe not.

To develop the concept of a residential rehabilitation center, the Society initiated a project in 1966 to research need and glean suggestions from the disabled community. Robert Lovering and Bob Schwanke headed the study, concluding that a comprehensive rehabilitation center would help young adults become functioning members of society. That same year, 1966, the Society started a special fund with a stock gift from Malcolm and Gray Mackay of Long

Lake as an incentive for the development of a new residential rehabilitation center. By 1968, that fund had reached $90,000.

The Society also faced the challenge of finding larger office space and funding growing programs. In 1960 it purchased and remodeled a former auto display building at 2004 Lyndale Avenue South in Minneapolis for $90,000. Expanding services put a financial strain on the Society as well. The increased Camp Courage budget plus commitments to the rehabilitation centers and equipment loan program created a demand for more income. Still tied to an annual mail campaign, the Society began to consider some alternatives. The mail campaign was costly and time-consuming and drew limited donations. Furthermore, a percentage of contributions had to be sent to the National Society for Crippled Children and Adults. Other funding sources had to be explored.

In 1961 community leaders in Minneapolis and St. Paul organized the United Fund to increase accountability, efficiency, and economy in the fund-raising arena. Replacing the Community Chest, it soon became the Twin Cities' major, comprehensive fund drive. United Fund leaders invited the Society to become a charter member, and the board of directors accepted, believing it a more effective and economical means of raising operating funds. Because the National Society for Crippled Children and Adults opposed affiliation with united campaigns, the affiliation between the Minnesota Society and the National Society ceased in 1962. This action mandated that the Society shape its own future in both program and fund-raising, a challenge it willingly accepted.

Independence brought new challenges and opportunities, particularly in the area of fund-raising. While the United Fund provided steady support and helped stabilize funding of services, it did not cover all operating expenses or any capital needs. The Society had to create new sources for funds to make up

Ninety-one-year-old Joe Cavanaugh of New Hope, the oldest camper at Camp Courage for many years, especially enjoyed fishing. Here he is assisted by counselors Pat Donnelly and Linda Duepner, in the 1970s.

for the annual mail campaign. It developed "Crippled Children's Appeal" door-to-door campaigns in areas with no united fund and applied to united campaigns in other major cities in the state. Within five years it was included in the campaigns of more than 340 cities. By 1964, its income exceeded half-a-million dollars for the first time.

Joseph R. Klawitter joined the staff in 1962 and was named director of community services in 1963. He and his staff organized Courage Appeals, negotiated with united funds, recruited county chairs, and served as liaisons with outstate communities. Klawitter looked back in 1988: "We gained an important presence in the communities. It was a two-way street. It let people know about our services and enabled them to let us know about their needs." The county chairs enlisted volunteers in each community. In 1967 Jane (Mrs. Kendall) Houlton of Elk River and Peggy (Mrs. Roger) Zehren of Winona were chairs of the new "Ambassador" program, meant to give volunteers more responsibility.

Jaime Head (center) and friends share fun at a day camp in Duluth, in 1988.

The community services staff also organized and coordinated day camps throughout the state, recruiting leaders and providing training for them. The first day camp was organized in Austin in 1961 at the suggestion of board president David Wick of Albert Lea, to provide close-to-home camping experiences for young children with disabilities. Today, day camps are held in 31 communities in 5 states, with nearly 600 children aged from 5 to 14 involved. Children attend camp daily for two weeks, usually at a local or state park, and enjoy outdoor activities and adventures that, for many, are first steps toward a regular session at Camp Courage.

JANE HOULTON: WE'RE NOT ASKING AS MUCH AS SHARING

I became county chair in 1952, not long after moving to Elk River as a 22-year-old bride. About two or three years later I became a board member. The board was trying to obtain land for Camp Courage, and there was no question the camp was going to be built.

When the camp was completed we had to have campers, and we didn't have a network for recruiting them. There was a lot of resistance on the parents' part to allowing a handicapped youngster who had never been away from home to go to camp for two weeks. So one of the things I did as county chair was to actively promote the camp within the county—going out and speaking to groups and clubs and churches about it. I called on the Sherburne County nurse, and she started to let me know about children who might want to go to camp. Sometimes I would go to rummage sales and buy shorts or swim suits or towels for campers who didn't have them.

Wilko Schoenbohm kept us all motivated. He had not only had the vision of what could be done but also the confidence to lead the way. Ed Meierbachtol was important to me, too. He was great at getting people to give things to Camp Courage—that's why he got the "Scrounger's Award" one year. His approach was to say to someone he thought could help, "I'm going to give you the biggest opportunity you've ever had. I'm going to let you in on something wonderful." I think that's the secret of it. We're not asking as much as sharing an opportunity.

Volunteer Jane Houlton has been involved with the Courage Center organization since the early 1950s, wearing the hats of county chair, Ambassador, vice-president and board member, chair of rehabilitation and vocational rehabilitation committees, Courage Auxiliary president, and coordinator of countless special events. By 1988 Houlton's cumulative total volunteer hours at Courage Center (from the time record-keeping began in the mid-1970s) reached 9,674.

7 Mergers and Affiliations

In the 1960s and early 1970s the Minnesota Society for Crippled Children and Adults, also known as MiSCCA, broadened the scope of its services considerably through mergers and affiliations.

In 1968, Curative Workshop merged with the Society, adding medical rehabilitation to the programs. The workshop's services included occupational therapy, physical therapy, home services, family services, a therapeutic preschool, speech and hearing services, and psychosocial services. The Society assumed financial and administrative responsibility of the workshop, but it had no space for the services, so the workshop remained at 18th and Chicago in Minneapolis. In 1973, it moved to the newly completed Courage Center and became the medical rehabilitation and education department.

Dean B. Randall of Minnetonka, a member of the Curative Workshop board, described the merger:

> The Society saw a need for a fully integrated organization in which a therapy program could be a big asset. The workshop approached us, and the chemistry was right. Curative Workshop was a small organization, making it difficult to expand or get any of the ancillary help needed. Physical therapy was becoming accepted in the medical community, and the hospitals were starting to set up their own physical therapy departments. The future of free-standing physical facilities was tenuous. So we joined the Society.

Signing the merger papers uniting Curative Workshop with the Society in 1968 are (standing) Dean Randall from the Curative board; Wilko Schoenbohm, executive director of the Society; Ruth Sherman from the Curative board, and Ed Meierbachtol, president of the Society board.

Established as a department of the Visiting Nurse Association in 1931, Curative Workshop had been funded by the Junior League and the Community Chest. In 1938 it moved to a new building at 2515 Nicollet Avenue in Minneapolis, and in 1949 it withdrew from the Visiting Nurse Association to incorporate with its own board of directors. The same year, with the help of the Society, it added a preschool for cerebral-palsied children. Curative Workshop relocated to 18th and Chicago in Minneapolis in 1957, and during the next 10 years added complementary services, including an amputee clinic, a work-hardening unit to help injured workers re-enter the job market, visual-motor perception testing, and homemaker's training.

Longtime director Margaret Adamson (1958-1969) had defined the emphasis on serving the needs of the whole person, a concept developed by her successors, Phyllis Rodrick Healy (1969-1984) and Diane Cross, current director of the medical rehabilitation and education department at Courage Center.

A second merger took place in 1968 when Minnesota Homecrafters joined the Society, reassociating with the organization that founded it in 1934 as the Lone Craftsman program. The service provided craft training in the home and helped market products made by disabled artisans.

The Lone Craftsman program had become independent of the Society shortly after it was founded and since 1947 had been supported by training fees from the Minnesota Division of Vocational Rehabilitation and Services for the Blind. Jean Conklin of Bloomington, former board member of Courage Center and director of Gillette Hospital for 27 years, was on the board of Minnesota Homecrafters at the time of the merger. She explained:

George DuBois of Minneapolis works on wood products for the Courage Homecrafters program, in the early 1980s.

Minnesota Homecrafters was so small—it wasn't really working the way it should. It didn't have the money for the kind of program that should be done. I thought we should do something, so I asked Wilko Schoenbohm whether he would be interested in discussing a merger. Lucille Maun from St. Paul, one of the Society's board members, set up a lunch for board president George Williamson, Schoenbohm, and me, at which a merger was agreed to and some details worked out.

In January 1968, the Society moved the program, renamed Courage Homecrafters, to a small, red house at Reindeer Square, on 44th and Chowen in Minneapolis, then being developed into a community of craft-oriented shops. The program moved in 1973 to Courage Center, where a giftshop was opened with proceeds from the raffle of a needlepoint rug created by Gray (Mrs. Malcolm) Mackay, of Long Lake, and several of her friends.

The program drew on the resources of the Society for administrative, promotion, funding, and volunteer help. In an effort to increase sales and outreach, Homecrafters opened offices in several outstate communities, subsequently closing them because of cost and lack of referrals. On a trial basis, the Society opened giftshops in downtown Minneapolis (1977), downtown St. Paul (1980), and Wayzata (1982) to market items made by artisans with disabilities. All three were later discontinued in favor of increasing sales in homes and at shopping centers.

As Courage Center services expanded, space became scarce, with the result that Homecrafters moved its offices and workroom to 1100 Zane Avenue North in Golden Valley in 1981 while the giftshop remained at Courage Center. As part of the vocational services department created in 1985, the program began broadening its scope to include home-based work other than crafts.

The program provides a valuable outreach to individuals, many of them living in rural areas, whose disabilities keep them out of the marketplace. Although earnings are usually not large, the income gives artisans dignity and self-worth. A key element in the program is the commitment of volunteers who staff sales, prepare materials, act as couriers, and provide social contact with the artisans.

Olga Aune enjoys crafts at Camp Courage, in 1968. Disabled from osteogenesis imperfecta and hearing-impaired, she stays active in her hometown of Frazee, where she was named Outstanding Woman of the Year in 1980-81. Aune visited Margaret Bradley in Minneapolis in the early 1970s to get some pointers on doll-making, and they continue to make dolls and other items for Courage Homecrafters.

MARGARET BRADLEY: BEING CREATIVE KEEPS YOU YOUNG IN SPIRIT

Margaret Bradley of Minneapolis has been designing and making dolls and animals for Courage Homecrafters since the 1940s. She learned to sew stuffed toys at Glen Lake Sanatorium, where she spent several years with tuberculosis of the hip and spine. At age 88, she still finds the creative process exciting:

I've made all kinds of animals—giraffes, cats, dogs, whole barnyards full of animals for children. I won many first prizes at the Minnesota State Fair with these. One of my favorite creations is the Red Riding Hood doll with three faces—Red Riding Hood, Grandma, and the Wolf—a best-seller for Homecrafters. My newest is a mother doll on her knees holding a baby high in the air.

I think that if you are creative you need never be bored. Even on sleepless nights, if you have problems, you can plan on working them out the next day. Being creative helps you keep up with the times. It helps you keep alert and active and young in spirit.

A third merger took place in 1974 when the Minnesota Handi-Ham System joined the Society to become the Courage HANDI-HAM System. The program had begun as an individual volunteer effort. In the 1960s, Ned Carman, an employee of the Mayo Clinic and radio officer for Rochester-Olmsted County Civil Defense, helped a neighbor with disabilities get radio equipment and a license. He saw the potential for opening the world to severely disabled people through short-wave radio and began encouraging others. Carman enlisted friends in the effort, including Ward Jensen of Minneapolis, who helped raise funds and interest supporters.

Once they had launched the program, Carman turned for more help to the nuns of the Franciscan motherhouse at Assisi Heights near Rochester. They quickly adopted the project, identifying and encouraging potential members to join and supplying them with equipment. Among those helping was charter member Sister Alverna O'Laughlin, now educational services director of the Courage HANDI-HAM program at Courage Center.

In 1967, Carman turned to the Society for help with the quickly expanding program. The Society responded with financial assistance and equipment, later appointing a staff liaison to work with the group. Bruce Humphrys was the appointed liaison. He explained:

> When I first became involved in 1972, there were about 50 members, almost all of them in the southeast Minnesota area around Rochester. Only six members were in the Twin Cities area. HANDI-HAMS became affiliated with Courage Center in 1969 and merged in 1974. That's when I became the director of the program.

Ned Carman

Ned Carman died in 1972, and the next year the system moved into its new Courage Center headquarters, growing to 250 members during the first two years.

In 1972, the system held its first Camp Courage radio camp, designed to bring together aspiring hams from all over the nation to study, practice, and pass examinations for licensure. It has been repeated every year since, at Camp Courage or Courage North. As the number of members grew, so did the staff. In the late 1970s Richard Eichorn, who had lost his sight because of diabetes, became Courage Center station manager, a position he held for about 10 years. In 1981, two staff members were added: student coordinator Maureen Pranghofer, blind since birth, and Sister Alverna O'Laughlin.

In 1981 Radio Camp traveled to Malibu, California, for its first West Coast session, now an annual event sponsored by Richard Steele of Newport Beach, California. Steele became interested in the HANDI-HAM program when a friend who was blind became a member. Margaret (Mrs. Reuel) Harmon of St. Paul funded the taping of instruction materials for vision-impaired hams and made a major gift to help perpetuate the program, while Albert T. O'Neil of Lake City, a ham and volunteer with the program since 1967, left a gift of $10,000 per year in perpetuity to Courage HANDI-HAMS.

The Courage HANDI-HAM System of amateur radio is now an international network of 7,200 members, including about 3,500 disabled hams and 3,700 volunteers. Members in 38 countries keep in touch through the Courage Center headquarters, and the system helps individuals with disabilities become licensed operators by providing:

- study materials and a counselor for each student
- loans of safe, high-quality, amateur radio equipment
- adaptations of equipment when needed for ease of control
- a worldwide fraternity of members
- support through the link with Courage Center headquarters
- a newsletter sent to each member.

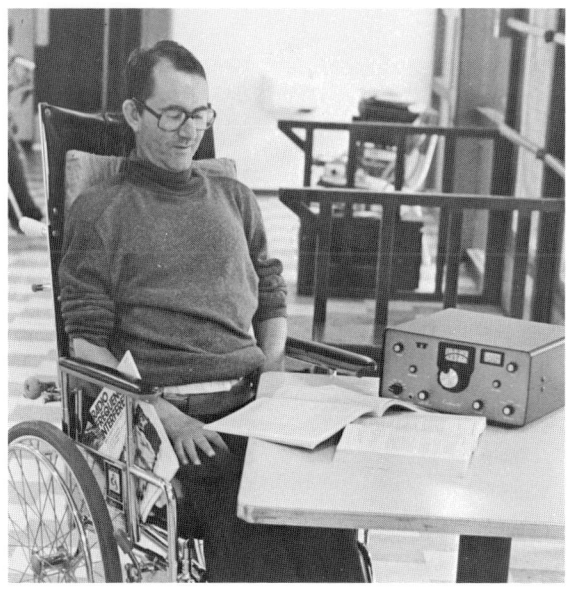

LeRoy Ljungren of Wadena studies for his extra-class license at a 1977 radio camp. Paralyzed from polio, Ljungren operated his system with a mouthstick.

MAUREEN PRANGHOFER: PEOPLE NEED TO KNOW THERE'S HOPE

I've been a member of Courage HANDI-HAMS since I was in high school, and I'm now student coordinator for the program, responsible for new people entering the system. I really enjoy my work.

Courage HANDI-HAMS and Courage Center have been a big part of my life. My mother was county chair back in the 1950s and 1960s, when the organization was called the Minnesota Society for Crippled Children and Adults. I attended Camp Courage every summer until I was 17. After college I went back to camp for a session and ran into Paul Pranghofer, a camper I hadn't seen since I was 10. I'll never forget the first time I met him. He was in a breakfast-cereal-eating contest and he ate 12 boxes of frosted flakes!

Paul and I were married in 1978. We have had some adventures, with our combination of disabilities. I am blind and Paul was born without arms and with one short leg. He has learned to use his feet for almost everything. He does all the yardwork and has a large vegetable garden.

We have strong religious beliefs, and that has helped us get through the difficult times. I am writing a book about our life and our faith to share with others who might be having a hard time. People need to see that even with problems there is hope.

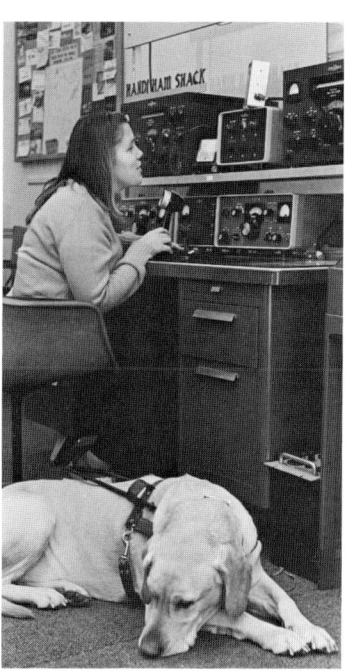

Student coordinator Maureen Pranghofer, with her dog, Kelly, keeps in touch with aspiring amateur radio operators all over the world.

Rolling Gophers Dan Sandstrom (left) and Wayne Anderson (blue and white) in a 1973 tip-off.

A fourth merger took place in 1977 when the Twin Cities Rolling Gophers joined the Society. The roots of wheelchair sports in the area went back to 1949, when the Minneapolis chapter of the Disabled American Veterans began playing basketball for fun, in space made available by the Naval Air Base. They attracted other people who wanted to get into the games, and the team became more organized, calling itself the Rolling Gophers. The Gophers began playing exhibition games against able-bodied basketball teams seated in wheelchairs. They also participated in the first national wheelchair tournament before disbanding.

In 1962 wheelchair sports re-emerged in the Twin Cities as the Minnesota Wheelchair Sportsmen Club, whose members played basketball as well as participated in bowling and trapshooting. In 1968 James S. Olson, director of camping and recreation for the Society, began coaching a wheelchair basketball team called the Minnesota Spokesmen. He soon took the team to Iowa for its first competition with an established team, the Des Moines Road Runners.

With the end of the Vietnam war, many young, disabled veterans returned to Minnesota, and the Spokesmen were able to recruit younger, more enthusiastic players. In 1971 the team changed its name to the Twin Cities Rolling Gophers. Six years later it merged with Courage Center as the Courage Rolling Gophers. After the merger the Gophers entered a new era of competition in a variety of sports, chalking up victories and earning awards on a local, regional, national, and international level as they competed in sports including wheelchair basketball, track and field, swimming, and archery.

The Courage Rolling Gophers won two national invitational tournament championships and sent players to the U.S. men's team in 1976, 1977, 1979, and 1980. They captured titles in softball, track and field, swimming, and archery, winning more than their share of medals at the annual national wheelchair games and international events. In 1975 a group of women formed a basketball team, entering its first national women's wheelchair basketball tournament, placing third. In 1979, 1982, 1987, and 1988 the team captured the national title.

As more players and participants became interested, the teams have grown to include the St. Paul Rolling Thunder, Chippewa Valley Wheelers, Rochester Cowboys, and Twin Ports Flyers of Duluth/Superior. The teams raise funds for competition through special events. In 1981 the Minnesota Handicapped Skiers Association became the Courage Alpine Skiers, bringing years of experience in organizing skiing instruction and events for people with disabilities.

KAREN CASPER-ROBESON: A STORYBOOK LIFE

Karen Casper-Robeson easily swings herself from her sports wheelchair into an office chair, her muscles conditioned by years of participation in competitive and recreational sports. As one of two program directors for Courage Residence, she is responsible for a staff of four working in admissions, follow-up and discharge planning, and transition into the community. Casper-Robeson is a swimming, track, and basketball champion, longtime camper, and Courage Center staff member since 1978. She has won several national awards in addition to her sports trophies, including the "outstanding youth" award from the March of Dimes and the Spurgeon Award for Achievement:

I developed cancer of the lymph glands when I was nine months old. People diagnosed with it then typically did not survive, and at one point, doctors said I had just six months to live. The tumors did nerve damage to my spinal cord, so I had to use crutches and a wheelchair to get around.

I've always had lots of family support. I went swimming and belonged to Campfire Girls and attended public school. But when I started attending Camp Courage at about age eight, I developed a different kind of confidence in myself. Other campers were disabled too, and I felt like one of the group. I was Camper of the Year and enjoyed that.

In 1972, Jim Olson said to me in his gruff, good-natured way, "Well, Casper, you know you should get into sports. If you're any good, you might be able to travel." I hadn't been integrated into physical education in school, but I had some underdeveloped abilities in swimming. I went into a weight-training program in tenth grade to get in shape, and that spring I went out for track with the Rolling Gophers at Courage Center. The next year, 1973, I went to my first regional in swimming, racing, and field events. I did well in wheelchair racing and swimming. I went on to national competition and international competition, participating for the next 10 years. I traveled—to Peru, Brazil, Mexico City, England, Nova Scotia, and Holland, and around the United States. Last summer, I was inducted into the Hall of Fame in New York—that probably captures all of it!

Participants in the groundbreaking for Courage Center, in 1971, are the Reverend L. Donald Bond of Mankato, former board president; Kevin Bobleter of St. Paul, who attended the therapeutic preschool; Margaret Bradley of Minneapolis, a Courage Homecrafters artisan; and Donald Bond Jr. of Mankato.

God, let your spirit be among us as we dig in the earth. We are not here for a burial, but a planting, and what we plant is a dream whose time has come. Grant that even as it dies as a dream that it may begin to come to life again as a reality. It is our faith that the hopes and loves which have inspired the visions within us will have their fulfillment in a more abundant life for those of your children who, through something not of their own choosing, have been cut off from what we so easily accept as our human heritage. Let faith nourish continued growth; let hope blossom in beauty as a widened fellowship: let love bear fruit in service and creative concern. God, this beginning is yet without form; but already, because your Spirit broods over it, we know there will be a new revelation of what things are possible to your people, who believe that because there is a need to be met, there is a response to be found.

THE REVEREND L. DONALD BOND

8 The Courage Center Dream Comes True

The Society held onto its dream for a residential rehabilitation facility that would enable it to bring growing programs together and give new impetus to the goal of helping individuals with disabilities live more independently. The special fund had reached $90,000 in 1968, still far short of financing a new center. Still, the board proceeded to work on plans for the center, defining these areas of need:
- children's rehabilitation
- adult rehabilitation
- residential unit with living and learning facilities for severely disabled young adults
- vocational services
- administrative area
- recreation, including a gymnasium and pool

In December 1968 came a stunning surprise that would make the dream of a "Courage Center" a reality. James Beaton, associate executive director of Courage Center, remembered:

> In the fall of 1968, when Wilko Schoenbohm was out of town, I received a call from John Rippe, an attorney in Caledonia. He informed me that a client of his from Eitzen had died and was being buried that day, and that he had left a substantial amount to the Society. I asked, "Is 'substantial' $10,000, $50,000 or $100,000?" He said, "At least." Well, Mr. Bunge left us more than a million dollars, most of it in stocks.

Benjamin Bunge had learned about the Society through his niece, Ann Griffith, Houston County chair for the Society from 1953 to 1959. Bunge was a 74-year-old bachelor, one of 16 children. He lived simply in several rooms of his 17-room homestead, using an old wood range in his kitchen and a potbellied stove for warmth in his living area. In one corner, a big iron safe was stuffed with more than $900,000 in blue-chip stocks. The safe was never locked, and neither was the house. Bunge lived a life of thrift and simplicity, making wise investments in land and stocks and bonds, increasing many times over the inheritance of real estate he had received from his parents, Mr. and Mrs. Christian Bunge Jr., pioneer residents of Eitzen. He took pride in planning to give most of his wealth to charity, and he was as good as his word. Except for nominal gifts to relatives, the bulk of his estate went to the Minnesota Society for Crippled Children and Adults.

The Society gave an old store and post office (once operated by Benjamin's father) on the Bunge property, to the Houston County Historical Society. It also gave a grant to Caledonia's Camp Winnebago for multiply-handicapped and retarded children, for a memorial cabin in honor of Bunge. It placed $100,000 in

Dedication speaker Julie Nixon Eisenhower greets Courage Children of the Year Jill Carstens of Clearwater and Michael Goad of St. Paul. At the dedication, in 1973, Eisenhower said, "The fact that Stage I of this Center was entirely underwritten by volunteer contributions tells more about your personal concern for peple with handicaps than anything else."

the Courage Foundation and the rest, nearly $1 million, in the Courage Center building fund. Staff and board members began making concrete plans for the new center. Beaton recalled:

> Mr. Schoenbohm set up task forces to define needs and space, and Joyce Vincent coordinated them. We did the work after our regular workday—we didn't mind because we all felt so positive about it. I marvel at how well we were able to design and construct Stage I of Courage Center, considering we had no blueprint to go on—there was no other place like it.

The Society searched for a site for the new center, and in 1969 it purchased seven-and-a-half acres overlooking Theodore Wirth Park in Golden Valley, from Glenwood Hospital (now Golden Valley Health Center) for $180,000. To augment Benjamin Bunge's legacy, the board approved a capital fund drive of $1,400,000 in September 1969, based on estimated costs of $2,450,000 for the facility. That early figure grew to $3,401,000. The board decided to build Courage Center in three stages, with Stage I including administrative headquarters, a gymnasium/auditorium, an unfinished pool area, and space for all the programs. Stage II would add the long-awaited transitional, independent-living residence for young, severely disabled adults and would complete the pool. Stage III would add space for growing programs and an educational center and expand the parking, kitchen, dining, and lobby areas.

Representatives of the Society broke ground for Courage Center on April 23, 1971. A cornerstone ceremony took place October 25, 1972, marking the completion of Stage I. The staff moved in December, and the center officially opened in January 1973. Courage Center was a reality, and the fund-raising goal had been reached as well: the building was paid for when it was dedicated in April 1973 with a week-long series of events.

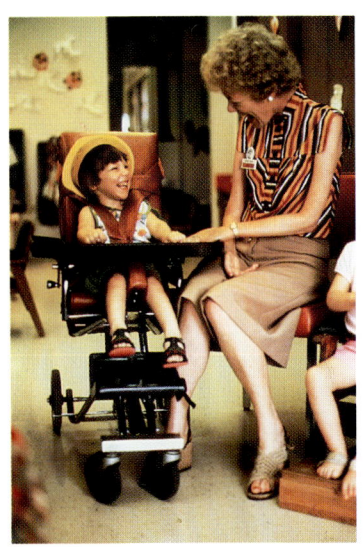

Volunteer Betty Held shares some fun with Kari Wagner in the therapeutic preschool, in 1981.

BETTY HELD: A JOURNEY OF DISCOVERY

Betty Held of Buffalo symbolizes the journey through disability to independence experienced by many people at Courage Center. Polio struck in 1954, leaving her with a damaged respiratory system, a paralyzed right arm, and limited use of her left arm and hand. It also left her dependent on her husband and two daughters for dressing, cooking, and transportation. Feeling helpless and unneeded after her daughters left home for college, Held turned to Courage Center. On the phone she said, "I don't know who I want to talk to, but your name is Courage Center, and I guess I need some courage."

Through participation in a seminar on attitudes toward disabilities and counseling, Held began to see herself in a new light, discarding attitudes that had burdened her for years and clearing the way for her to move ahead. She explored and used many Courage Center services: counseling, occupational therapy, painting classes, and a rehabilitation engineering service that designed and built a "dressing tree" so she could dress herself. And she learned to drive using foot controls.

As Held's confidence grew, she began reaching out. She volunteered in music therapy with preschool children, became a tour guide and speaker, headed a volunteer management committee, and was named to the board of Courage Center. Today she coordinates the Sherburne-Wright County adult handicap program, which provides lifelong learning activities to adults with disabilities. She serves as an elder in her church and as a member of the Minnesota Community Education Association. In 1988, she was honored for her achievements with a Rose and Jay Phillips Award.

9 Courage Residence

The completion of Stage I of Courage Center:Stage I brought a tremendous explosion of activity. For the first time, with a broad range of services under one roof, the whole person could be treated, not just a disability. Services included physical and occupational therapy, speech and hearing services, counseling and family services, recreation and sports, camping, a therapeutic preschool, life enrichment activities, amateur radio, craft training and merchandising, and more. The building, which had seemed so big when the staff of 70 moved in, was bulging by 1974, when fund-raising began for Stage II—the addition of a pool and Courage Residence.

Preschooler Erica Riley of Minneapolis tries out a new toy with the aid of therapist Kaye Bedhauer, in 1983.

The shell of a planned swimming pool had been built during Stage I, for completion when funds became available. In 1974 generous gifts from Fred C. and Katherine Andersen and the Andersen and Bayport Foundations made completion of the pool possible. The pool opened in the winter of 1975, launching a program of therapeutic and recreational swimming that would benefit thousands of children and adults.

The opening of Courage Center also brought budgeting challenges. In 1972, the last year at 2004 Lyndale Avenue, the organization's budget was about $720,000. As the result of the move to Courage Center and the expansion of programs and activities, the budget grew to $1,000,000 in 1973. Several factors helped close the gap between income and expenses:
- increased public donations because of visibility and reputation
- substantial growth in contributions of $1,000 or more to the annual Guardians of Courage fund, under the leadership of development director Lee Berglund
- increase in fee reimbursement income in medical rehabilitation services, spearheaded by department director Phyllis Rodrick Healy
- the addition to staff of an experienced controller, Lawrence S. Johnson

These combined efforts resulted in solid growth in income, greater cost-effectiveness, and better accounting. With the new systems in place, staff and volunteers turned their attentions to the development of Stage II: Courage Residence. Jim Olson, director of camping, recreation, and residential services, and Margaret Anderson, Minneapolis artist disabled by polio, led the detailed planning for the residence. According to Olson:

> The concept for Courage Residence was to provide an environment that would bridge the gap between hospital care and the community, to help people get their living skills up to the point where they could live independently and their vocational skills up so they could get involved in the marketplace.

The residence would be as homelike as possible. Rooms would be cheerful and bright, with balcony or patio to allow residents to enjoy the beautiful setting. Aides and nurses would wear street clothes rather than uniforms. The environment would be relaxed and caring. Above all, residents would be treated with dignity, as individuals. They would define their own goals and make contracts with staff to work toward them. They would take responsibility for their own plans and progress.

With $900,000 raised toward a goal of $1,750,000, ground was broken in June 1974, and construction was completed in January 1976. During the next month, 64 young men and women from all over the nation moved in to begin a

Courage resident Dan Baustian of Jasper practices independent living skills, in the 1970s.

unique experiment in independent living. For a dedication ceremony in April 1976, young people living in Courage Residence chose Barry Hite of Emily to represent them and receive a symbolic key to the new facility—a "key to a new day." At the dedication he flourished the key above his head in triumph, expressing the exhilaration of planners, builders, donors, and residents alike.

Residents represented a variety of disabilities, including spinal cord injuries resulting in quadriplegia or paraplegia and disabilities such as cerebral palsy, polio, muscular dystrophy, and stroke. They came from restricted living environments such as hospitals, care centers, and nursing homes, or dependent living situations with their families. At Courage Residence, they were challenged to take steps to improve health and strength, reach an understanding of their disabilities, and define their futures. They responded by achieving more than they had believed possible.

The original concept that Courage Residence would provide long-term housing for many severely disabled adults, with training and work opportunities on the same site, quickly changed. The skills they were learning—how to hire and direct an attendant, how to manage checkbook and bills, how to understand medications, how to dress and feed themselves—were vital tools for living independently. And the tools worked. According to Mark S. Moilanen, associate executive director of programs:

> When Courage Residence was planned, the concept of people with severe disabilities living independently was really a dream. In fact, the original concept was that something like 40 percent of the residents would have to live there permanently because they would have no opportunity to live on their own.
>
> Not long after the residence opened, staff realized that philosophy was not appropriate because almost all the people, given the right services, could live independently. Our thrust shouldn't be to house them forever, but to provide services and advocate in the community for more accessibility so that they could have that opportunity.
>
> Residents demonstrated that they could live independently, and they began moving out faster than we could accommodate them. We were all so excited when they began moving into the community—it was great. People who had been in institutions for years or at home with Mom and Dad for decades were now on their own. The pride—the sense of accomplishment!

For the first time, individuals with severe disabilities were becoming citizens in every sense of the word, thanks to an environment that was becoming more barrier-free each year and a public that was recognizing the importance of making jobs and housing available to all its citizens. Individuals with disabilities were working, paying taxes, buying homes, marrying, and having families, just like everyone else.

The development of Courage Center coincided with the opening of society to people with disabilities. In *The Quiet Revolution*, James Haskins wrote:

> In the 1960s a quiet revolution began to spread across the nation, spearheaded by disabled activists and their supporters. Disabled Americans started to come out of their pockets of isolation to band together to fight for the cause they hold in common—the elimination of the prejudices and discrimination that have prevented them from leading lives of dignity and independence. They have been presenting their case in the courts, lobbying their legislatures and publicly demonstrating for the removal of all the physical, social, legal, and economic barriers to their enjoyment of full citizenship.

The . . . civil-rights movement of the 1960s spurred the efforts of these groups. Like blacks and other minorities, disabled Americans also suffered from prejudice, discrimination, segregation, personal degradation and economic deprivation—all of which contributed to the denial of their basic human and legal rights. As one disabled activist put it: "Blacks were relegated to the back of the bus; we can't even get on the bus."

The same year that Courage Center opened, the most important piece of federal legislation relating to employment of disabled individuals was enacted. Section 504 of the Rehabilitation Act of 1973 prohibited discrimination against individuals with disabilities "under any program or activity receiving federal financial assistance." It mandated that all government agencies and any business, school, or organization receiving more than $2,500 in federal money must take "affirmative action" to hire and promote individuals with disabilities.

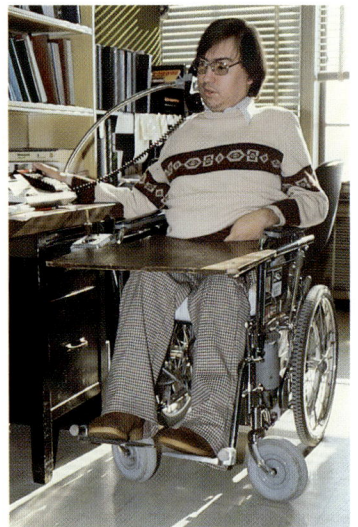

RONALD G. TUURA: IT ALL CAME TOGETHER

Ron Tuura has used a wheelchair for mobility since age 13 because of muscular dystrophy. In 1976 he was living in a nursing home in Superior, Wisconsin, his hometown, unable to find suitable housing: "There was one other young fellow there. He was going to school. He went home for the summer and then it was just old people there. There was the usual recreation—weaving baskets and that sort of thing—but nothing real meaningful. It was a comfortable place for ending a life, not beginning one."

Tuura had earned a bachelor's degree in engineering from the University of Wisconsin in Milwaukee and had found an engineering job in Duluth that lasted just nine months, cut short by economic recession. In 1976, he learned about Courage Residence from Max Rheinberger of Duluth, applied, and was accepted. He moved in in February, the first day the residence opened, and lived there until December 1977: "The encouragement I got at Courage Residence was really important. Before I came here, nobody really expected anything of me. You get complacent. It provided an atmosphere for getting back into life, for being a person again. At the residence, it all came together."

The day Tuura moved out of the residence was a landmark in more ways than one. He and Nancy Howes, a cook in the Courage Center kitchen, were married. "She's still cooking in our kitchen," he laughs.

Tuura became something of a legend by driving his new, battery-powered electric wheelchair 16 miles to Met Stadium for a baseball game—twice. Using Courage Center transportation and newly developed interviewing skills, Tuura applied for 20 jobs in 18 months before being hired by the Science Museum of Minnesota in St. Paul as resource coordinator. Soon afterward, he was hired as a civil engineer by the U.S. Army Corps of Engineers, a job he has held since. The Tuuras and their two children—Carly 6, and David 4—live in northeast Minneapolis.

10 Courage North

Courage Center had a landmark year in 1971. Ground was broken for the Center, and Courage Auxiliary, a new volunteer organization supporting Courage Center, held its first event. In addition, St. Paul shopping-bag entrepreneur Walter H. Deubener and his wife, Lydia, notified the organization that they were donating their north-woods summer home to expand camping opportunities for people with physical disabilities and speech, hearing, and vision impairments.

In 1898 Walter Deubener was a 12-year-old orphan in Waterloo, Indiana. Ten years later he was a grocer, who with his wife, Lydia, ran a cash-and-carry store in St. Paul. "Many times a day I would notice that a customer's purchases were limited by what she could carry rather than by her pocketbook," Deubener said. One night, a thought flashed across his mind: Why not a large bag, with strings through and around the bottom for support and carrying handles at the top? Thus was born the modern shopping bag, an industry, and Courage North.

In January 1972, the Deubeners officially bequeathed their summer retreat at Lake George—a 95-acre, lakeside, pine-filled site with a house and several cabins—to Courage Center. The Center organized a pilot camping program for teenagers with severe hearing impairments at the new site. According to Robert L. Polland, camping director since 1977:

> Courage North's character—rustic, in the north woods near Itasca State Park—lent itself to outdoor "outward bound" activities for young people with hearing impairments. The idea for a "leadership camp" for teenagers grew out of experiences at Camp Courage when we held a special session for campers with severe hearing loss, separate from the speech session. We realized that profoundly hearing-impaired or deaf teenagers have few opportunities to develop leadership and grow in self-confidence, so we planned an experimental 12-day wilderness camping session at Courage North. It was a neat beginning, and it set the tone for Courage North.

The main goal was to get teenagers with hearing impairments to be responsible for their own actions and to plan their own activities.

The leadership program is a key part of Courage North today. On the first day of the session, campers select a council to represent them and choose a schedule from a list of committees and activities. Each camper receives a "checkbook" and an explanation of the banking system. The checkbook contains $100 in imaginary funds. With these, the campers must pay for all special activities and keep their checkbooks balanced. If they overspend, they go to work—cleaning, repairing, and gardening—to earn credits. The credit system provides a visual, material record of the value of work and the importance of carrying out responsibilities. For some campers, it is the first opportunity to do so.

Walter and Lydia Deubener at "Deep in the Pines," their summer home at Lake George, in the 1940s. Walter Deubener posted many signs around the site, one of which advised, "He who chops his own wood warms himself twice."

Tom and Mimi Fogarty live in the log home built by Walter and Lydia Deubener as a summer retreat. Tom, director of Courage North, is hearing-impaired. He attended Camp Courage and later worked as a counselor there. He also met Mimi at camp, where she was a counselor, too.

Although Courage North's rustic facilities were adequate for a limited number of campers with hearing impairments, Courage Center wanted to open it up to individuals with physical disabilities as well. In 1976 the staff and board made plans to expand the facilities by adding several winterized, log buildings: a dining hall/leadership facility and six cabins. They also made plans to build wheelchair trails through the wooded site and to develop the beachfront area. The additions increased Courage North's capacity from 16 to 48 persons per session.

With good funding response from individuals and organizations, expansion was well underway by 1977. The dedication of Courage North took place July 15, 1979, and the expanded camp opened in June 1980. Today, Courage North sessions serve four main groups: hearing-impaired children, deaf teenagers, campers with physical disabilities, and children recovering from burns.

Teenagers with hearing impairments at a 1975 leadership session at Courage North head out on an overnight hike.

11 Decade of Growth

The completion of Courage Center in 1973 launched a decade of unprecedented growth in programs and services. Existing programs expanded in the new facility, and many new services grew in response to demonstrated needs. Courage Center's strength was its flexibility as a private entity. Its leaders could initiate programs in response to need if funding could be arranged through public support or grants from foundations or corporations. Now, in a decade of change, Courage Center was put to the test as staff and board focused on the emerging needs of people seeking to live more independently in the mainstream of society.

Not only was the environment permitting disabled individuals more freedom of movement, the disabilities were changing, too. Polio, once the leading cause of disability, had been conquered with the development of the Salk and Sabin vaccines, though postpolio clients continued to need help. More children were surviving the perils of premature birth and birth injuries, diseases such as cystic fibrosis and cancer, and conditions such as spina bifida. More adults were surviving the trauma of stroke and accidents, and many faced years of living with disability. Treatment of disabling conditions improved, adding years to the lives of people with diseases such as multiple sclerosis and muscular dystrophy.

A new population group emerged: individuals with head injuries, most of whom had survived accidents. Escaping what would have been certain death even 10 years earlier, many individuals, most under 30, experienced severe intellectual and emotional trauma. Many were unconscious for months following their accidents. One effect was that Courage Residence began to receive applications from individuals with brain injuries from all over the nation. Chris Duff, program director of Courage Residence, explained how the program developed:

> We were one of the first facilities in the country to provide community-based rehabilitation for people with brain injuries. There were few models. We tried to look at the unique needs of individuals with brain injuries and devise programs to meet those needs. We instituted memory strategies, such as "life books," in which the individuals wrote all their appointments and other important information. We helped them develop the systems they needed to function, like memory logs, daily structures, and repetition.
>
> When we started, most of the rehabilitation community thought we were wasting our time working with people who had been injured for more than a year-and-a-half. The thinking back then was that there would be no further recovery after that point. We know now not only that there is more recovery but also that people can learn ways to compensate for their injuries. The brain is one of the few parts of the body that does not regenerate itself. But we can teach the brain to use other pathways to accomplish similar functions. Individuals can compensate for the loss in their cognitive processes.

Courage Center's medical rehabilitation and education services also expanded in the new facility. Curative Workshop brought a solid structure of services including therapy, psychosocial services, speech and hearing services, and a therapeutic preschool. The goals of the department remained unchanged: to increase clients' independence at work, at school, at home, and in the community, through increasing strength, reducing pain, improving communication skills, and gaining skills for daily living.

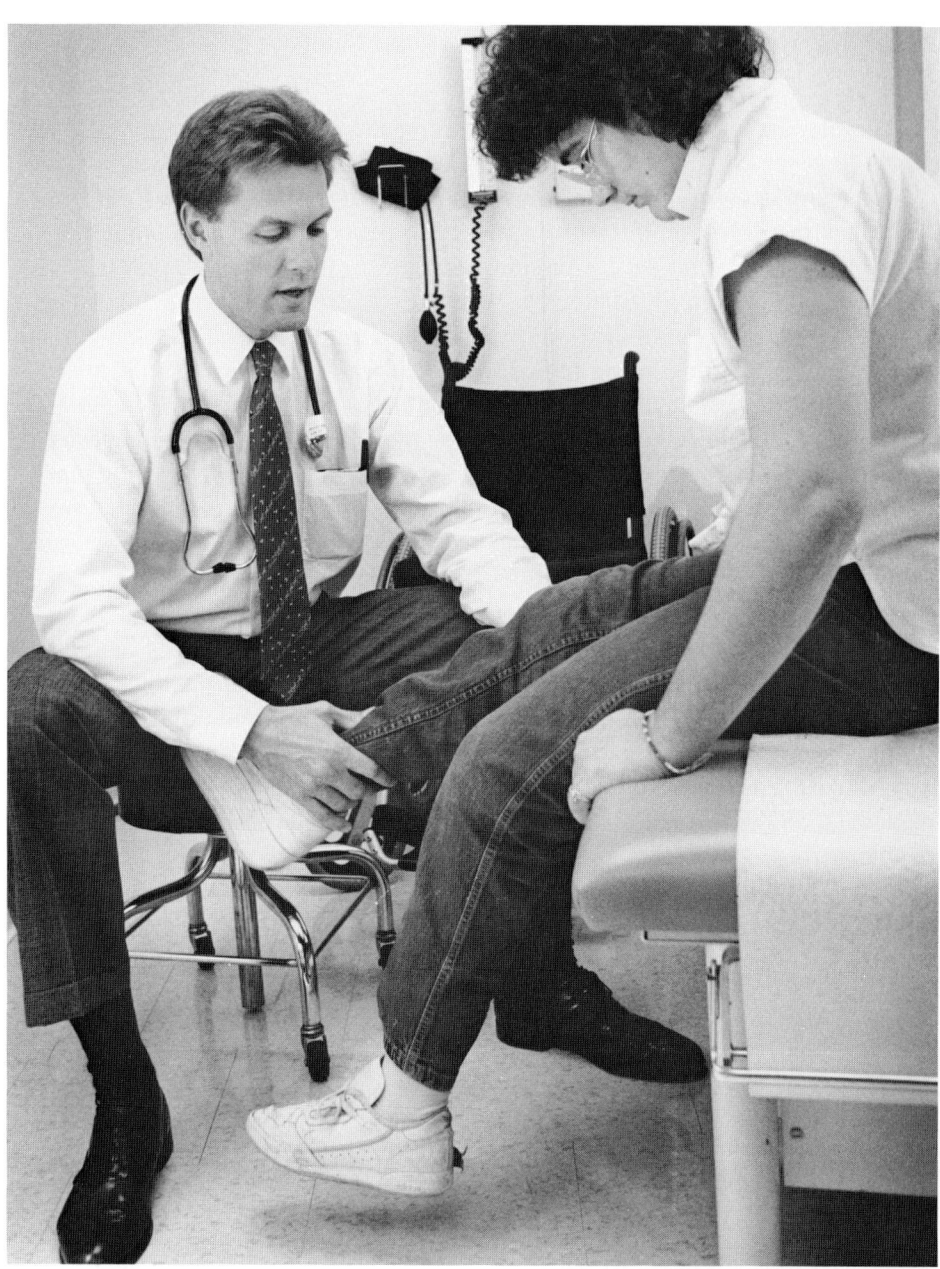

Medical director Mark Moret examines resident Michelle Boyle of Moorhead. Physicians Ronald Bateman and Arthur Quiggle, longtime associates of the Center, also serve Courage clients.

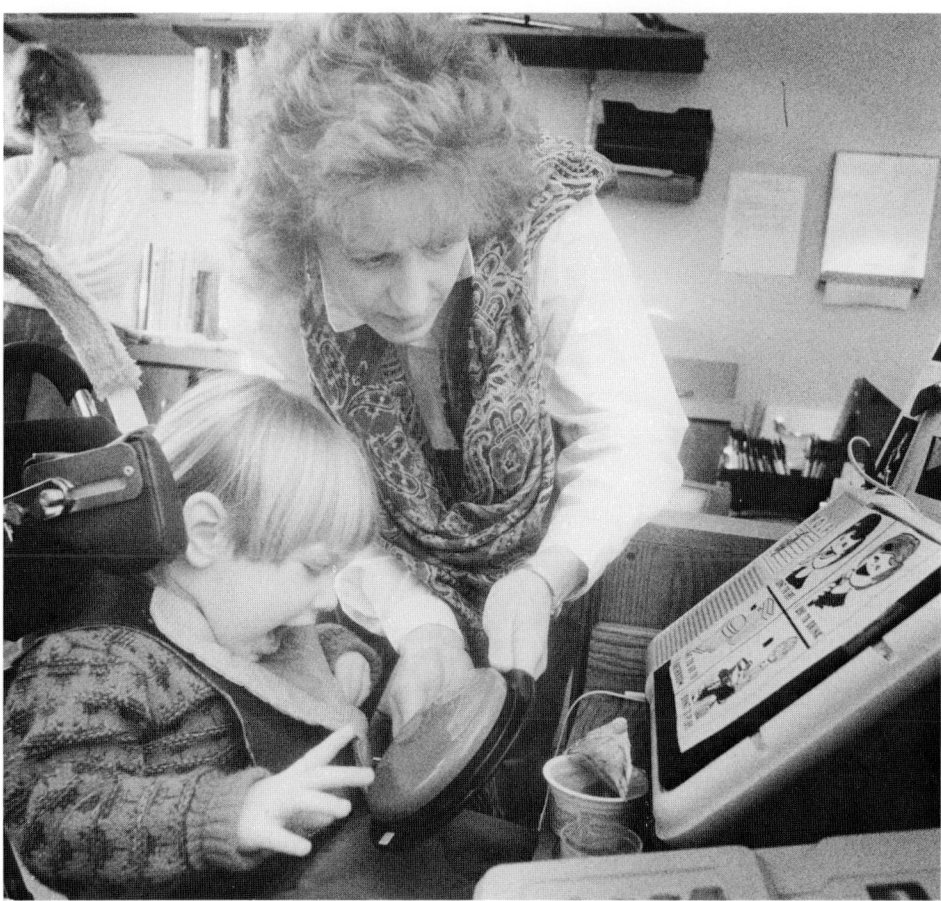

Lindsay Dressen of Big Lake tries out an augmentative device to improve her speech, in Courage Center's communication resource center. Helping her is speech therapist Mary Beth Ingold.

Staff members expanded the team approach, including:
- physiatrists (physicians) specializing in problems of neuromuscular disease or injury
- physical therapists helping clients develop strength and mobility through exercise, heat therapy, and gait training
- occupational therapists helping clients develop fine motor skills and independent living skills such as eating, dressing, writing, cooking, and hygiene
- speech/language pathologists and audiologists providing evaluation, testing, and therapy to help overcome hearing, speech, and language problems. The staff also operates a communication resource center enabling individuals who cannot speak to explore alternative methods of communication through devices ranging from simple alphabet boards to sophisticated electronic speech aids that "talk" for the person.
- clinical social workers providing assessment, consultation, program management, and counseling to individuals and groups
- special education teachers working with children under age four to provide classroom experiences integrated with prescribed therapy

Bobbie Vickerman and Julie Trebtoske of Minneapolis enjoy a swim in Courage Center's pool, in 1976.

The department of sports, physical education, and recreation also flourished, with completion of the gym and pool setting the stage for tremendous growth in the number of individuals participating and activities offered. Courage Center support of aquatics went back to 1958, when the Minnesota Society for Crippled Children and Adults joined the American Red Cross in sponsoring "learn to swim" classes for disabled children. Classes were held at Fairview Hospital in Minneapolis and later in St. Paul, Rochester, St. Cloud, Marshall, Grand Rapids, and Faribault. And swimming had been a vital part of the camping program. Courage Center's therapeutic pool opened in 1975, thanks to a generous gift from the Andersen and Bayport Foundations. Its special features to accommodate people with disabilities included a roll-out deck with water filled to the edge for easy access and a ramp for wheeling into the pool. The water's temperature was set at a soothing 92 degrees Fahrenheit.

Bobbie Vickerman was involved for more than 30 years in teaching aquatics to people with disabilities, first as a Red Cross volunteer and then as Courage Center's aquatics program coordinator. She left that position in 1988 for health reasons and was succeeded by Marcia Bevard Kulick, longtime participant in the center's competitive sports programs, including swimming, basketball, and wheelchair road-racing. Kulick currently holds 7 of 12 world records in swimming. Vickerman spoke in 1988 of her involvement in Courage aquatics:

> My goal has always been to get people to enjoy the water as much as I do and to get them to feel better about themselves and others. I've watched a lot of kids grow up since I started as a volunteer. We went from a simple recreational swimming program to therapeutic aquatics, and from a handful of participants to 37,000 in 1987. The program has changed a lot of lives. When we started taking clients with stroke, arthritis, and other disabilities, doctors heard about the program and sent more to us. Now there are three physical therapists in the program.

It's been so rewarding to see people enjoy the pool. I learned early on how to take someone who was disabled on dry land and teach them how to maneuver in water. I noticed that people could leave crutches, canes, and chairs and have wonderful freedom in the water with alleviation of pain. A child who could not move much out of the water, with the support of the warm water, could do something that increased his self-confidence. Seeing a child grow is the only reward I ever want.

Today the pool is used daily for a variety of activities such as family swimming, scuba classes, "water babies" for children six months to three years, individual instruction, inner-tube water polo, water volleyball, swimnastics, aerobics, stroke groups, and arthritis groups.

Another popular program, Perfect Squares, a wheelchair square-dancing group, grew out of recreational activities at Camp Courage in the early 1970s. Warren Berquam and his wife June, of Maple Plain, organized the Perfect Squares in 1975, and the group has performed to rave reviews locally and nationally. In 1978 the Berquams organized a second group, the Midnite Squares, for people who are legally or totally blind. The Berquams have chalked up more than 5,700 hours as volunteer leaders and callers. Warren said, "The positive results of what we're doing have been written on the faces of every audience that's seen us perform. We're not getting their sympathy—we're being recognized for something we do just as well or better than they do!"

For youngsters from 7 to 14, Courage Center formed the Saturday Club in 1975 to provide opportunities for self-motivation and self-direction. The children manage their own budgets as they plan field trips and activities at Courage Center and in the community. Young people outgrowing the Saturday Club later established the Teen Club to continue their involvement with group activities.

TONY LEBAHN: I'M A REAL COMPETITIVE GUY

Tony Lebahn, Courage Center's client services representative, likes people—especially those he has met since becoming involved with the recreation program at Courage Center. Lebahn, who also likes sports, joined a floor hockey team in 1974. Born without arms or legs, he held the stick between his chin and shoulder. He used a similar method in 1978 when he took on violinist Itzhak Perlman in a game of foosball. Perlman was visiting Courage Center before performing a concert to benefit the life enrichment program. He challenged Lebahn and went down in defeat. "I'm a real competitive guy," Lebahn explained.

Lebahn learned survival skills early, growing up in a family of four boys: "If I was pushed down by one of my brothers while wrestling or something, I had to figure out a way to get myself up, so I learned to kind of flop myself up like a rocking chair. Or I'd use my chin to grab hold of a couch and pull myself up. I always told myself I was on the same level as others and could compete with them at different things, even simple things like turning pages in a book, playing cards, or swimming. My mom and dad always encouraged me to do things for myself as much as I could, but they were always there if I needed something. Some things were frustrating, but I always kept on trying until I succeeded or came up with an alternate plan."

Lebahn's early learning experiences were augmented by a stay at Courage Residence. Lebahn, his wife Terry, and their two children, Casey age 4, and Jason age 1, live in New Hope.

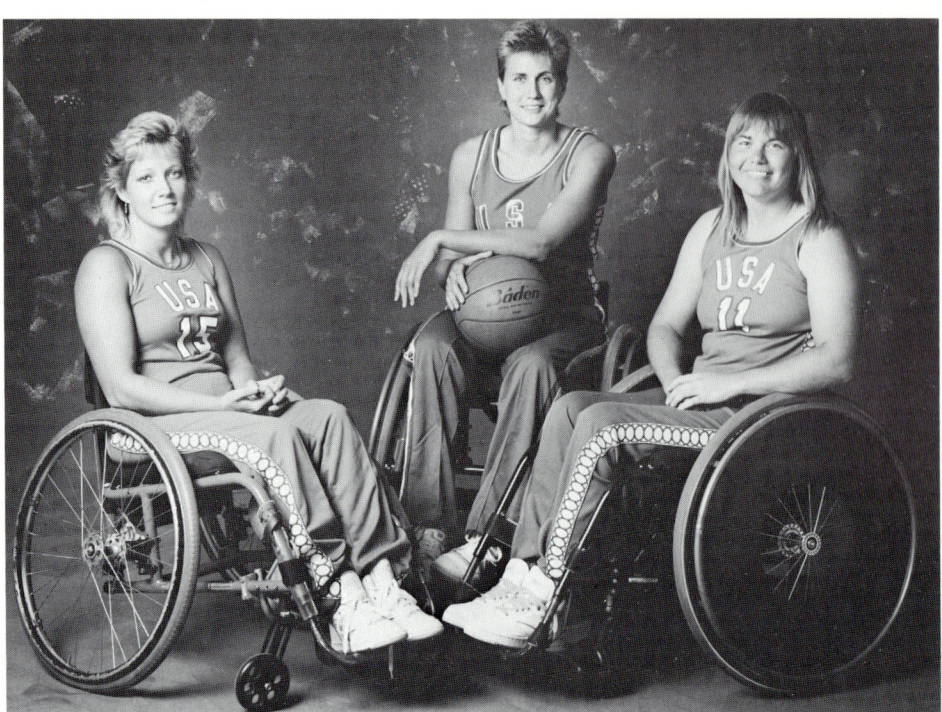

Paralympic gold medal winners Mary Ann O'Neill of New Hope, Debra Sunderman of Savage, and Sue Hagel of New Hope.

Michael Anderson of Crystal, member of the Courage Rolling Rascals, throws the discus, in 1981.

An array of recreational and competitive sports developed at Courage Center, including basketball, track and field, swimming, softball, table tennis, weight-lifting, football, floor hockey, skiing, and archery. The department added the Rolling Rowdies program for people from 10 to 18 years old, and the Rolling Rascals for younger children. In 1983 Courage Center launched an annual junior invitational wheelchair basketball tournament, attracting teams from throughout the United States and Canada to compete in the Camp Courage gymnasium.

Courage Rolling Gopher teams have gained international recognition. At the 1988 international Paralympic Games in Seoul, Korea, three members of the Courage Rolling Gophers women's wheelchair basketball team played on a U.S. team, capturing a gold medal. In addition, Rolling Gopher Tami Oothoudt of Minneapolis won the marathon gold, setting a new Paralympics record, and Mike Stauner of Golden Valley won a bronze medal in the men's short metric archery event.

In 1979 Courage Center demonstrated its commitment to people with hearing impairments by hiring full-time staff coordinator Harvey Hoffman, who is profoundly deaf. He directs a sports and recreation program reaching almost 300 individuals. Activities include volleyball, swimming, co-ed sports, touch football, pool tournaments, basketball, bowling, and floor hockey. Children from 5 to 10 years old can join a Cub Scout pack, Brownie troop, or adventurer's club at Courage Center.

Established in 1979, Courage Center Duluth Area Services provide sports and recreation opportunities for children and adults in the Duluth/Superior, Wisconsin, area, including social and recreational activities, competitive sports, and fitness programs.

Volunteer Robin Lampert of St. Louis Park, leads Courage Center Cub Scout Pack #264, whose members are hearing-impaired.

ROBERT J. SZYMAN: EVERYONE DESERVES THE OPPORTUNITY

Bob Szyman became director of the new sports, physical education, and recreation department in 1978. He reviewed department progress in 1988:

There has been a lot of growth since 1978. At that time, 525 people were involved in the program. That figure has grown to almost 2,400. Courage Center was the only site for sports and rec in 1978; now we're in the east metro area, northeastern Minnesota, Duluth, Grand Rapids, and Biwabik, as well as in Eau Claire, Wisconsin. The budget in 1978 was $250,000; in 1988 it's $818,000. Volunteer hours given to the program totaled 2,100 in 1978; now it's 14,715. In 1978 fees were collected from only a few; this year 20 percent of our revenues comes from fees.

The Rolling Gophers men and women have done a lot to increase the visibility of people with disabilities and to change people's attitudes. They are models for other disabled individuals. A major goal of our department is to give boys and girls an opportunity to grow, through experiencing some of the frustrations of life. One of the reasons kids with congenital disabilities have a tough time making the transition from school to job to community is that nobody helps them acquire a true picture of themselves and the world around them. Instead they are helped at every turn. Even when they are allowed to make decisions, others might intercede to make sure it is a positive experience. How can they find out what works or measure themselves in comparison to the rest of the world without some failures? Everyone deserves the opportunity to succeed or fail in his own right. The structure of our department helps get people to the point where they can make their own decisions.

Our ultimate goal, like that of other programs at Courage Center, is meaningful integration. There is some progress. Some of our kids are swimming in regular swim meets, and the Minnesota Amateur Sports Commission state games now include people with disabilities. Some high schools have given letters to kids involved in Courage Center sports. We want to help educate recreation providers that with proper coordination, people with disabilities can participate in their own communities and not be separated from their friends.

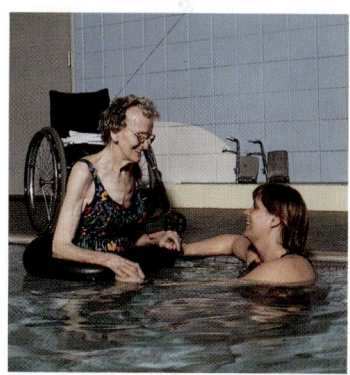

Marcia Bevard Kulik encourages Lucy Wilichowski, 93, of Marathon, Wisconsin, to exercise in the 92-degree water.

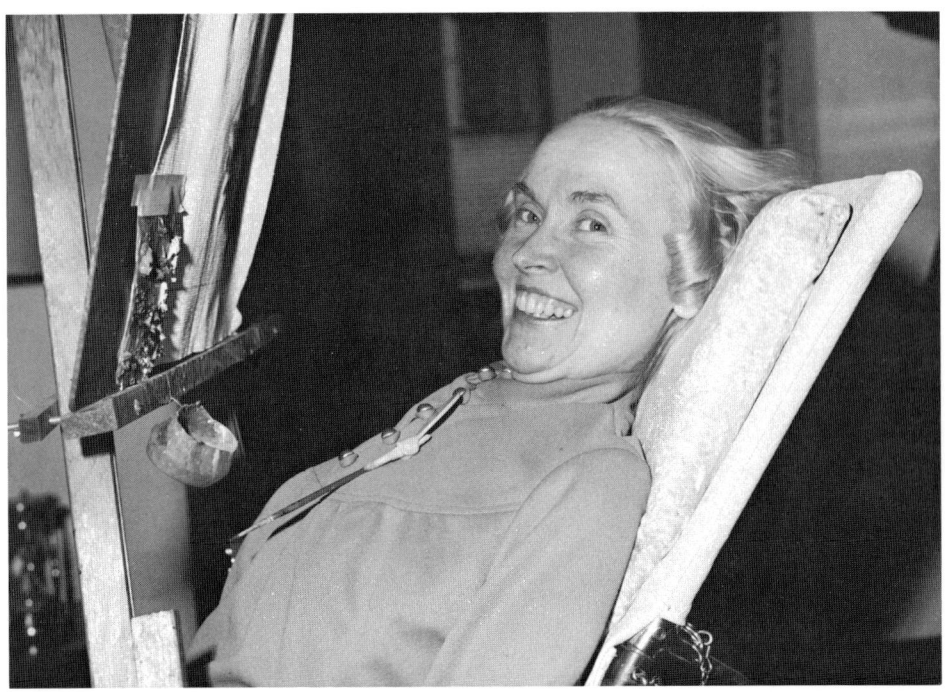

MARGARET ANDERSON: A COURAGEOUS SPIRIT

Margaret Anderson, well-known Minneapolis artist who was paralyzed from polio, helped plan Courage Residence and served as its first administrator. At the time of her death in 1977 of pneumonia, she was Courage Center's life enrichment coordinator.

Anderson was an inspiriation to those who knew her. Dependent on a respirator, she nevertheless led an active life. She launched the Sister Kenny International Art Show for Disabled Artists and the Sister Kenny Auxiliary. She operated a successfurl needlepoint design business and enjoyed painting, which she accomplished by holding a brush in her mouth. In 1973 she received the Rose and Jay Phillips Award as one of Minnesota's outstanding disabled individuals. Margaret Anderson left an enduring legaacy, summed up by these words: "God sends love in so many different ways—the gift of a new day, the gifts of a child, knowledge, friends, and nature. These all become treasures—to store and translate into creation. I believe God gave each of us a body to let us discover, taste, and express life. After the body stops growing, it is time to develop the spirt."

12 New Programs for Changing Needs

In addition to experiencing tremendous growth in its existing programs, Courage Center added new services during the 1970s and early 1980s. One such program was life enrichment classes. Like everyone else, individuals with disabilities need the stimulation of new activities to grow in self-awareness and confidence. Unlike everyone else, disabled individuals cannot always attend community classes because of architectural barriers, transportation difficulties, and communication problems.

Shortly after Courage Center opened, it initiated Courage Classroom, a 15-week pilot program offering a variety of classes to disabled individuals. By 1976, students were attending classes in music, art, writing, amateur radio, dancing, astronomy, sign language, theater, wheelchair repair, and hand-control driving. Subjects added later included assertiveness, sexuality, and self-awareness.

According to Cynthia A. Raynor, coordinator of life enrichment classes since 1980:

> Life enrichment classes serve a very real need for people with disabilities to be involved and to broaden their world. Since 1982 we have been taking classes into the community to provide greater access. In 1987 we took classes to 10 accessible sites, such as senior apartments or nursing homes in the Twin Cities area. Our total participation is 1,300 individuals, up from about 100 in 1979.

Alyce Bergey of Lanesboro, Minnesota, and Elvin Haley of Amery, Wisconsin, create paintings in a life enrichment class in 1982.

We charge a modest fee for classes—it increases student commitment. Only about one-third of the participants are able to pay, so we count on endowment funds and donations to make up the difference. Most instructors are volunteers who come forward with an interest and offer to teach it.

Life enrichment classes were for adults only until 1986, when staff organized after-school classes for children at Courage Center.

Courage Center's music therapy program began in 1977 with grants from the St. Paul Schubert Club and Robert A. Schmitt Foundation and a bequest and memorial gifts in honor of former board member John Rogers of Dellwood. According to Cindy Raynor, coordinator:

> Rehabilitation professionals have long recognized the value of music in helping individuals express themselves and gain understanding of their feelings and emotions. The goals of music therapy are to increase integration, fine motor development, growth in understanding of concepts and numbers and colors [used to identify notes], and receptivity and expression—and to have fun. For adults, music is a social ice-breaker, a form of discussion. There is a lot of satisfaction in singing in our chorus or joining in a musical jam or just playing an instrument by yourself.

Staff members adapt instruments or tools when necessary, sometimes with the help of rehabilitation engineers and shop workers. Some changes are simple,

Scotty Lloyd of Minneapolis discovers the fun of a music therapy session at Courage Center, in the mid-1980s.

such as restringing an instrument or using large notes and a keyboard labeled to match for someone who is visually impaired. Some are more complicated, like a guard for the autoharp to help the player strike just one key at a time.

Cindy Christiansen of Minneapolis brought her daughter, Mycah, who had the use of just one hand, to the music therapy staff for help in 1984. She wrote:

> We recently consulted Courage Center for help in adapting a violin for my child. Not only did they adapt the violin for her, but they gave her several lessons of instruction on how to play it. My daughter is now confident of her abilities . . . and is presently enrolled in Suzuki instruction.

Art therapy for adults was added in 1982. It differs from life enrichment art classes in that it defines specific goals for participants, such as expression of feelings. It is also less product-oriented. "People can often express painful things through art," coordinator Cindy Raynor said. "It can help them strengthen self-confidence and improve self-esteem."

One new program at Courage Center grew into the national Courage Stroke Network. The concept of a stroke support group was developed in the early 1970s in Texas, and the first Minnesota group was formed in 1972 at the Mankato Rehabilitation Center. Nurses in the Ramsey County Health Department initiated the first Minneapolis/St. Paul stroke group in 1974, inviting stroke survivors and spouses to start a club. Maxine Haarstick of Minneapolis and Marcella Sotebeer of St. Louis Park chaired the Twin Cities steering committee. Their husbands, Wally Haarstick and Orville Sotebeer, were stroke survivors. Wallace Haarstick, known locally for portraying Abraham Lincoln, had been getting therapy at Courage Center, and the group began meeting there.

The group formally organized in 1975, electing Wallace Haarstick president. It split into St. Paul and Minneapolis groups in 1976, and by 1979 seven active groups existed in Minnesota. Maxine Haarstick, recognizing the potential for growth and service, asked Courage Center for help in coordinating the groups' efforts, and Robert F. Lepp, director of psychosocial services, took on the project on a part-time basis. Volunteers helped with phoning, a newsletter, mailing lists, seminars, peer counseling, and other tasks.

JUSTIN KARON: A STROKE DOES NOT HAVE TO BE THE END

Shortly before his death in 1987, Justin Karon said:

It has now been 12 years since my two cardiovascular accidents—strokes . . . first a minor one, then the one that left me completely immobile on my left side. When I first became alert after days of immobility in a hospital bed, my left side was gone, but I could move a finger on my left hand. I said, "I'm going to walk out of here," and I did, three months later. Progress was slow but steady. Still, I was not and never will be completely restored physically. Mentally—that is a different story.

I became aware of the Twin Cities Stroke Club and made that contact at Courage Center. Since then I have become more and more involved in the program. I know now a stroke does not have to be the end. As a volunteer, I help develop new clubs and advise existing clubs in programming and other matters. The most important change to me is that when I leave Courage Center after my work stint, I leave stimulated, invigorated. Sometimes I walk out physically drained but alert, thinking, "What is ahead for tomorrow? Next week? What new idea can I come up with? How can this tremendous staff at Courage Center put another idea together?" And I feel good, being part of it.

The number of stroke groups continued to grow all over the nation. Jean Conklin, retired director of Gillette Hospital in St. Paul, provided coordination on a volunteer basis for eight months in 1979, guiding the network in its evolution from the Courage Stroke Club into the Courage Stroke Network. In 1987 the network got a major boost when Courage Auxiliary gave a grant to hire a full-time director, Pat Kasell. The Stroke Network now includes some 700 groups with 30,000 members, in every state. About 60 percent are stroke survivors, 30 percent are spouses or colleagues, and 10 percent are rehabilitation and medical professionals.

Courage Stroke Network offers information on stroke, referral to local stroke groups, assistance with organizing groups, the *Stroke Connection* newsletter, annual seminars, and outreach through peer counselors who visit individuals hospitalized from stroke. Local clubs or groups are organized independently, but find the network a helpful resource. Most groups meet monthly and schedule programs and speakers on subjects such as the stroke experience, community resources, medical services, coping, finances and family relationships.

Another new program, driver education, has been a key to independence for many individuals with disabilities. Mark Moilanen, associate executive director of programs, told how it began:

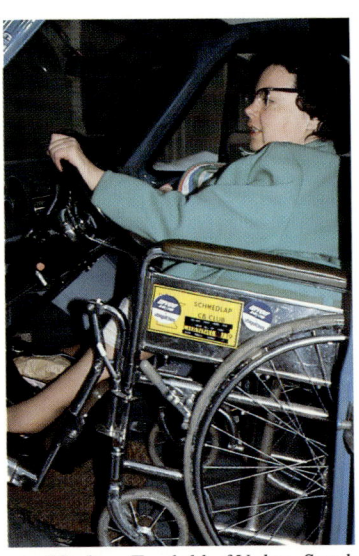

Merlene Tevdahl of Volga, South Dakota, learns to drive while living at Courage Residence, in 1979.

> Jim Olson, then director of camping, recreation, and residential services, asked me when I was residence program director in 1978 to investigate the possibility of a driver education program. We'd had a Courage Classroom session in 1974 in hand-control driving but no actual instruction. I found out driver education for people with disabilities was embryonic throughout the nation, so we developed a brief plan, and Jim took me in to discuss it with Wilko Schoenbohm. I brought up potential problems such as other organizations offering the same service. Wilko said, "Compete, don't complain." I mentioned some possible financial difficulties, and he said, "Do your best, trust for the rest." Then he flipped the paper back and said, "Do it!" Olson and I walked out and got busy.

David Nelson, director of driver education and transportation since 1978, described how it grew:

> There were very few models in the country. We used a donated van for a year or so, although its design was not entirely suitable. Then we ordered a second vehicle, and by that time technology had improved and we could get special features like a lowered floor, electric lift, and low-effort steering—50 percent easier than regular power steering. This made it possible to help people with more severe disabilities.

GAIL COLVIN: DREAMS DO COME TRUE

Gail Colvin of Hopkins wrote in 1982, after passing her state driver's test:

I have had severe rheumatoid arthritis since 1967 and was nearly totally bedridden for 10 of those years . . . For years I have read *Courage News* and once in a while I would see a mention of the driver training program at Courage Center. The articles planted a seed in my mind . . . When a person is sick for a long, long time, much of what keeps them going is dreaming dreams . . . One of my dreams came true today when I finished my driver's training with Dave Nelson and got my driver's license at the Plymouth exam station. It is a big step for me to be able to go somewhere on my own!

I hope everyone who is sick or disabled in any way will keep hoping and not give up. Sometimes it takes a long time, but dreams do come true.

The first year we opened the program to people in the community, serving about 30 residents and 15 outpatients in 9 months. As word spread, the program grew. At the end of 2 years we had served 125 people and added Steve Quinn as an instructor. He is now manager of the program. Within 3 years, the only other existing local program decided to contract with us. We now work with more than 400 clients each year, and we have served about 2,000 clients in 10 years.

The program serves Courage residents, people in the metropolitan area, clients at Courage St. Croix in Stillwater, and since 1982, 14 other cities in the region. The outreach program started with a call from Sioux Falls, South Dakota, asking us to consider bringing our service down for about five clients. We did, and then added Marshall, Rochester, and Duluth in Minnesota, and Bismarck in North Dakota.

The development of technology has helped the program work. We use a Doran driving simulator, a steering simulator, a visual-reaction-time tester, and a new "adjustable steering" test that determines whether a client can handle regular power steering, low-effort, or zero-effort steering. Our rehabilitation engineering service helps solve individual needs with special designs and adaptations, as the program prepares clients to pass the regular state driving test. Achieving that goal provides great freedom. A client can wheel up to the van, activate the door opener, lower the lift, get on the lift, enter the van, and wheel into driving position. The electric tie-down system locks the wheelchair in place. The client may put on a driving cuff to help grip the steering device attached to the wheel, before driving away.

Programs like music therapy and driver education led to another launched in the 1970s—rehabilitation engineering. Courage Center was the second major rehabilitation organization in the nation to establish a rehabilitation engineering program specializing in technology to help individuals overcome physical limitations and live more independently. The program began in January 1979 with the help of a grant from the Bush Foundation, following the recommendations of a rehabilitation engineering committee composed of engineers, scientists, industrialists, staff, clients, and volunteers.

Committee member and rehabilitation engineer Don Mauer, the first director of the program, was assisted by a dedicated cadre of volunteer engineers and toolmakers. Many of the group, still involved in 1989, were Honeywell retirees. Rehabilitation engineer Ray E. Fulford, who has directed the program since late 1979, said:

Because Courage Center is such a comprehensive rehabilitation facility with many activities and services, the program had the opportunity to address a wide variety of problems. For example, young men and women learning independent living skills at Courage Residence needed special tools and devices to help them become as self-sufficient as possible. And people with disabilities in the community did, too.

Some of the independent-living devices we invented or adapted were special hand or mouth controls for electric wheelchairs, silverware with modified handles for easier grasping, tools for handling controls on appliances like ovens, fixtures for stabilizing kitchen appliances like electric can openers, carriers for moving pans and casseroles into or out of the oven, T-shaped key handles, mouthstick holders, stabilized nail clippers with extended handles, stands for positioning telephones, and a special electric wheelchair seat that enables an individual to sit down and get up without help.

For life enrichment art classes, we made a powered easel, which tilts the drawing surface to vertical or horizontal. And for the recreation department, one item we devised was an archery bow-holder for individuals with reduced hand function.

Computers became part of the program soon after it was established. Resident Dan Hedberg of Lindstrom had broken his neck in a diving accident shortly before graduating from high school. A whiz at math, Hedberg wanted to explore a possible career in that field, but he did not have the strength or dexterity to write mathematical equations. Rehabilitation engineers suggested he try a computer and called Control Data with their idea. The company supplied computers and worked with Courage Center to help clients explore their use, and rehabilitation engineers devised a way for Hedberg and others to operate the computer with a mouthstick. Engineers also adapted computer controls for operation with limited hand movement, eye movement, and, in one instance, tongue movement. They fabricated keyboard guards for people whose spasticity made it difficult to hit just one key at a time and a disk handler for people with limited dexterity. Control Data continued to supply computers, and, impressed with the field's potential for disabled individuals, hired Dan Hedberg to help develop special programs for the company.

From 1979 to 1982, Courage Center operated a technological work evaluation program with a grant from the Federal Rehabilitation Services Administration. Its purpose was to find ways to help people overcome physical barriers to employment in high-technology industries. The program helped pave the way for disabled individuals to enter the computer age and laid the groundwork for a computer lab now being developed at Courage Center as part of the department of rehabilitation technology.

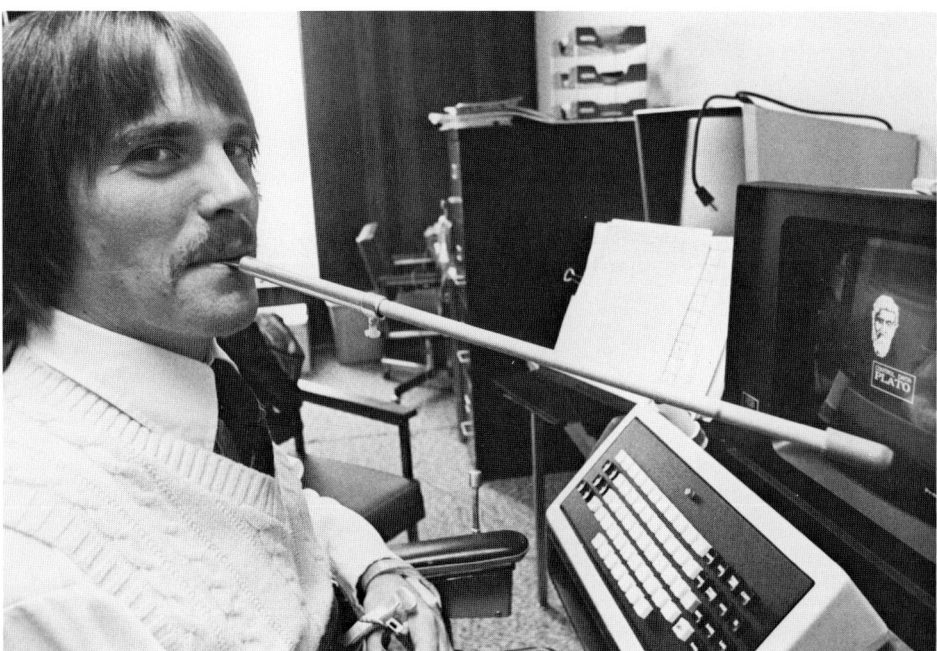

Dan Hedberg in 1979

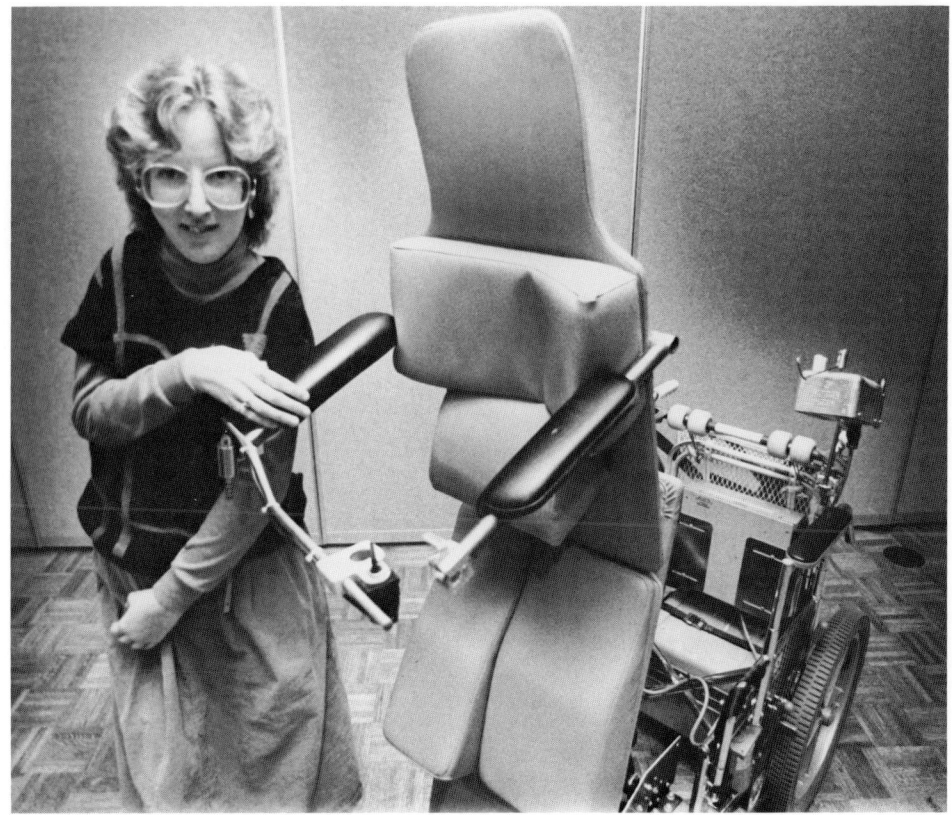

Rehabilitation engineers designed a special powered wheelchair enabling Mary Grimm of Minneapolis to stand up and sit down without assistance.

JONATHAN LESLIE: INDEPENDENCE IS THE GREATEST GIFT

In August 1977 when I was 19, I was involved in a motorcycle accident and broke my neck. I spent about seven months in North Memorial Hospital. When I got out I went through a lot of mental stress trying to decide whether I wanted to live or not. The thing that turned me around was that people cared about me even though I didn't care about myself. Relatives and friends all went on the line for me.

I was an outpatient at Courage Center for about a month, then I moved into Courage Residence in May 1978. One of the greatest things there was being able to see other quads doing things for themselves. All there was between me and them was months of work. And I did work hard, really hard, learning how to put on a shirt, use a buttonhook, lifting weights, learning to drive. I got my license in August 1978. By then, I was dressing myself and getting in and out of my chair. I now live in my own home in Golden Valley.

Courage Center gave me the opportunity for independence—the greatest gift there is. There was a lot of love and support from people, but Courage Center had the staff to help me. The independence I got at Courage Center allowed me to go back to school. At first I took one night class, then two day classes. I had to start at the beginning, with freshman algebra and trigonometry, then I went into calculus, physics, and so forth.

I graduated in mechanical engineering in 1985 and got a job with Slicer, a company in south Minneapolis, where I still work designing computers and writing software.

*Jonathan Leslie hunts ducks with special equipment—
a chair bolted to a pontoon boat, a sling to hold the gun, and a
trigger he can activate with his teeth—
that he designed himself.*

13 Winds of Change

In 1978 Courage Center celebrated its golden anniversary—50 years of service to people with disabilities. It also officially changed its name from the Minnesota Society for Crippled Children and Adults, Inc., to Courage Center. Staff and board launched a variety of activities to commemorate the occasion:
- a professional seminar on attitudes toward disabilities
- a benefit concert by internationally renowned violinist Itzhak Perlman to endow the life enrichment program
- an arts and crafts workshop in memory of Margaret Anderson, disabled artist, former administrator of Courage Residence, and coordinator of life enrichment classes
- publication of *Tributes to Courage,* a book of stories about 13 remarkable individuals with severe disabilities
- a golden anniversary endowment appeal, with the goal of expanding endowment from $250,000 to $5 million
- the "Courage Song" composed by Jeanne Smith of Minnetonka and performed at many programs and ceremonies

Three years later, the International Year of the Disabled called attention to the needs and achievements of disabled people all over the world. Courage Center marked the special year with educational activities, including the designation of a "Courage Sunday" in April, when churches throughout the region held programs on the topic of disabilities.

Another project was the building of a model independent living home across Golden Valley Road from Courage Center. The idea grew out of a suggestion by Jay Suel of New Prague, a member of the community relations committee of Courage Foundation. Because he used a wheelchair as the result of being disabled from multiple sclerosis, he enlisted Courage Center's help in making his home more accessible. Pleased with the help he received, he urged the Center to share its expertise with others seeking to make environments barrier-free. The demonstration home, built with the help of interested friends and foundations, was dedicated April 24, 1981. Home for three severely disabled individuals and their attendants, it serves as a model and resource center for people planning accessible housing.

The year 1983 marked a major change in Courage Center's leadership. After presiding as executive director over 31 years of growth and change, Wilko Schoenbohm announced in April that he would step aside at the end of the year and take on a new role as executive vice-president of Courage Foundation. D. Stephen Farley of St. Paul, president of Courage Center's board of directors, praised his work:

The Center's growth since 1952 from a staff of less than 20 to over 300 today, and from an annual budget of less than a quarter of a million dollars to over $7 million today, with no major debt outstanding, is a marvelous tribute to his resourcefulness. Wilko Schoenbohm's leadership and faith have made the Courage Center story possible and the dream of a better world for people with disabilities a reality.

Schoenbohm received several national and local awards, including the Distinguished Career Award from the National Association of Rehabilitation Facilities in 1981, the Minneapolis Rotary Club's first "Service Above Self" award in 1983, the Franciscan International Award in 1986, and honorary degrees from his alma mater, Wartburg College, and from Concordia College in Moorhead. Schoenbohm responded to the accolades with these words:

> As outstanding and as necessary as good facilities are, the glory of Courage Center must always rest not in its assets or investments, nor in its modern buildings, but in the hope and opportunity that its wide range of services are providing disabled people of all ages. I think we have demonstrated that as a community we do care about the needs of our fellow citizens. We must continue to do all we can to help those who struggle against disabilities share in our dynamic civilization and have a chance to take their place as a part of society rather than be kept apart from it.

The new executive director, David M. Hersey, took office January 1, 1984. President of Blake Schools in the Minneapolis area for nine years and previously associated with Macalester College in St. Paul, Hersey brought impressive

David Hersey

management skills to his new position. He led the board in developing a five-year plan for the organization and defining this mission statement:

> The mission of Courage Center is to promote the maximum independence, personal responsibility, and dignity of people who have a physical or sensory disability, with primary emphasis on individuals with severe or multiple disabilities. Courage Center provides, pioneers, and promotes vital and caring programs in rehabilitation, independent living, and recreation at the appropriate regional, national, or international level.
>
> Courage Center shares its knowledge and expertise with others who work with disabled persons and designs its programs to complement other services available. Courage Center promotes public awareness of the abilities and needs of people who have a disability to facilitate their full participation in society.

Chaired by Frank Madden of St. Paul, the planning committee defined these five-year objectives:

- expanded vocational services
- increased emphasis on technology
- increased services to people disabled by head trauma and to the disabled elderly
- focus on expanding some services regionally and nationally
- development of accessible housing and services in smaller communities throughout the region

---

LINDA MARZINSKE: YEARS OF COURAGE

Linda Marzinske of Brooklyn Park was a spokesperson for Courage Center for many years. She was a camper in the late 1950s, camp staff member in the late 1960s, and Courage Center public relations assistant in the 1970s. Born a triple amputee, she grew up in Albert Lea in a family that prized independence. She attended public schools, including the University of Minnesota at Morris, where she majored in public speaking. After graduation in 1971, she enrolled for a radio and television course at Brown Institute in Minneapolis, then began working for the Courage Center organization at Franklin and Lyndale in Minneapolis. In her five years with the Center, she worked as coordinator of volunteers and tours, receptionist, public speaker, and public relations assistant. In 1979, Marzinske won a Rose and Jay Phillips Award.

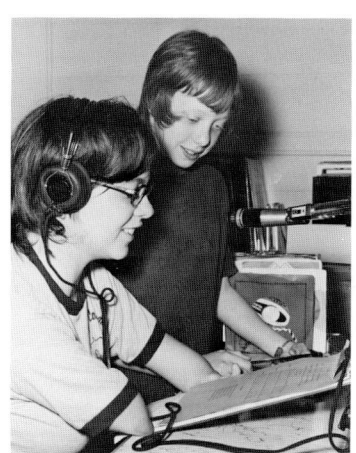

Linda Marzinske shows camper Leslie Mattson how to operate the Camp Courage radio station, in 1972.

Camp Courage was my first experience as a member of the disabled family. I especially enjoyed the overnights at Lake Koronis, where there were so many blue herons, and the "survival overnights" when we slept outside and ate food growing in the wild. I made so many good friends there.

During the summers while I was going to college, I worked at Camp Courage as kind of a "Girl Friday," greeting visitors, giving tours, working in the store, covering the switchboard and filling in for kitchen staff when needed. We had just opened the speech side of camp and Uncle Al was pretty busy—he couldn't do it all, so I helped out.

At Courage Center, I really enjoyed speaking to groups such as the Future Farmers of America and the United Way. At the time, there weren't that many people with disabilities speaking to groups or getting up in front of the public. They were still more or less kept at home. I found it was easier if I used some humor.

I have fond memories of Courage, but I knew it was time to move along. In 1977 I started working for Prudential as an education specialist, doing orientation for new employees, career orientation, time management, and some public speaking. I recently became training supervisor. And I'm still a volunteer speaker for the United Way.

David Phillips

- continuing emphasis on private, community contributions to support services so Courage Center could continue to serve clients regardless of their ability to pay
- cooperation with other health care agencies in the joint development of new services
- innovative use of Camp Courage for specialty programs
- further development of community recreation
- expansion of services for families affected by disabilities

David Hersey did not live to see the plans realized. He died suddenly of a heart attack in June 1985, and Jim Beaton, associate executive director of administration, took on the reins of leadership until a new director could be named.

In January 1986 David A. Phillips took office, bringing broad administrative and fund-raising experience to his new position as executive director. Phillips had worked with the University of Minnesota Foundation for seven years, including service as director of development. Previously he was executive director of the Metropolitan Medical Center Foundation and executive director of Youth Leadership, a Young Life training program. He was a member of his local school board and was named president of the Minnesota Jaycees in 1972-73.

Phillips holds a master's degree in divinity and a doctorate of ministry from Bethel Theological Seminary in St. Paul. His strong interest in social services has evolved naturally out of his background as the son of missionaries in China, where he was born. "The idea of working in something other than human services never crossed my mind," he said.

With a dedicated executive director at the helm and a future plan in place, Courage Center faced the coming years with confidence. One of Phillips's major challenges was to complete the fund-raising for the construction of Stage III.

In 1980, seven years after it opened, the Center had felt growing pains. Programs, staff, clients, and volunteers had grown almost fivefold, and lack of space limited many programs. Every program area was filled to overflowing. Clients enrolled in driver education took instruction in a converted tub room, students in life enrichment classes met on the gym stage or in the second-floor

---

LISA BARON: COURAGE EVERY STEP OF THE WAY

Lisa Baron has benefited from many Courage Center services. She was two years old when her parents, Joan and Tony, discovered Curative Workshop's therapeutic preschool, then at 1800 Chicago Avenue in Minneapolis. "I thought the preschool was the greatest thing for us as a family," Joan said. "We found out we weren't the only parents who had a child with cerebral palsy. We got a lot of support through the parents' club, and Lisa got a lot of help through occupational and physical therapy, speech therapy, and especially, socialization. She didn't have many children to play with in our neighborhood, and she learned in the preschool how to relate to other kids."

In 1973, Lisa began attending the preschool in its new location at Courage Center. As she grew older, she used some wheelchairs from the equipment loan program, joined the swimming program, attended Camp Courage, and joined the Saturday Club, a group of youngsters planning field trips and other community activities. She also learned to ski at a Courage Center clinic.

At South High School in Minneapolis, Lisa played on the adapted floor hockey and soccer teams and graduated with honors. She wanted to start college right away, but her parents suggested she spend some time at Courage Residence to gain some independent living skills: "The counselors at the Residence told me I should learn to plan ahead, to do more for myself and not to blame other people for my own failures. In the beginning I didn't want to believe them and wouldn't listen to them. But when I went to Southwest State for a functional evaluation, the counselors there told me the same thing. That was really hard to hear, but I know it helped me mature."

Before she headed off to Southwest State University in Marshall for a trial quarter, Courage Center rehabilitation engineers built a guard for Lisa's computer keyboard so she could touch just one key at a time. They also designed a swing-out bag for the back of her wheelchair and a lap tray for her books and equipment. At a positioning clinic, therapists made her more comfortable and stable by inserting a firm back in her chair.

At college in the spring of 1988, Lisa lived in a double room by herself to allow room for her special equipment, including a manual and an electric wheelchair and a computer for her studies and communication. She paid a notetaker or got copies of the instructor's notes. She earned a 2.7 average in her first quarter and she plans to continue.

Lisa returned to Camp Courage in the summer of 1988 for her tenth session. "It is really neat," she said. "I see all my friends from school and Courage Center, and some people I played soccer and field hockey against at South High." Lisa's mother added, "Courage Center has helped Lisa every step of the way."

Lisa Baron gets some tips from craft director Bridgett Johnson at Camp Courage.

corridor, visitors and tour groups watched a slide show in the first-floor corridor, and several closets were converted into offices. Programs and conferences in the gym forced the cancellation of recreational events. One program, Courage Homecrafters, moved into leased space near Courage Center.

Clearly, it was time to push ahead with Stage III plans for an addition that would provide room to grow and ensure income for programs through endowment. In 1980 the board approved a campaign for $6.715 million, including $3.715 million for capital and $3 million for endowment. Construction would begin when two-thirds of the capital goal was met. The addition called for 40,000 square feet more of floor space, including two floors above the existing dining area and a third floor above Courage Residence, enlarging the dining area, kitchen, and lobby, and improving the pool locker room.

The first floor above the dining room would house an education center, a flexible, multipurpose area with movable walls and state-of-the-art audio-visual capabilities, including infrared hearing equipment. The space would be used for classes, tour orientations, conferences, seminars, and professional presentations and would house Courage Institute, a planned educational outreach. Courage Auxiliary provided funds to construct and equip the education center, including a meditation room dedicated in memory of June (Mrs. Andrew) Darling of Minneapolis, a founder of Courage Auxiliary and former Courage Center board member. The second-floor addition would provide offices and workspace for growing services and space for the volunteer program and Courage Auxiliary.

Planning for the expansion hit a snag when the Center learned that a building permit would not be granted without enlargement of the parking area. Nearby Golden Valley Health Center agreed to sell an additional 3.3 acres of land to Courage Center, providing space for the construction of a 100-car parking lot and a new road to service the lot. To cover the new costs, Courage Center increased the capital fund-raising goal to $5 million in 1985. Construction began that spring and was completed in the summer of 1986, coinciding with successful completion of the fund-raising campaign.

The addition of Stage III completed the Courage Center headquarters, a concept that had begun with a dream in the 1950s and culminated with the completion of one of the leading rehabilitation facilities in the nation.

Phillips also continued to carry out the goals defined and initiated in 1984 by the Center's planning committee. The committee had made recommendations for stronger vocational services, greater emphasis on rehabilitation technology, and the establishment of the long-planned Courage Institute for educational outreach. From 1985 to 1989, board and staff members carried out these recommendations while redefining children's services, strengthening psychosocial services, and building its first satellite facility.

Courage Center created a new vocational services department in 1985, to provide a variety of career, training, and employment options, improve the employability of people with disabilities and educate potential employers about their capabilities. The Center had been supportive of vocational services since its establishment of the Lone Craftsman program in 1934. It supported the growth of a network of rehabilitation centers and sheltered workshops in Minnesota in the 1950s and 1960s, many of which offered extensive vocational services. In addition the organization provided on-the-job training for individuals. And in the 1970s, after the opening of Courage Residence, staff counselors worked with residents on vocational needs and set up a technical work evaluation program to help them explore computers as a vocation.

According to Michael Wirth-Davis, director of the department of vocational services, the Center recognized the need for better focus:

> Courage Center was doing a good job of preparing people to live independently and to enjoy recreational activities, but we needed more focus on what people could do with those productive hours and how they could parlay them into work activities for pay. The department rounds out the Center's services, adds a piece that was missing.

Hal Lance of Plymouth works on the computer.

The department developed several components: A career center provides information and training to help people make career decisions and develop skills to compete in the marketplace. Home-based services offer two options: Homecrafters, a craft training and marketing program, and Home Enterprises, noncraft employment options such as computer work, telemarketing, assembly, clerical work, and consulting. Another Courage Center-based program offers career awareness, work experience, and job exploration, drawing on various employment and volunteer opportunities.

Finally, community-based services provide work opportunities, including internships, in the community for people with disabilities. The vocational services department also administers the Bush Loan Fund, established in 1974 by the Bush Foundation and Courage Center to provide low-interest loans to help sheltered workshops throughout Minnesota finance contract work for their programs. Of the future, Wirth-Davis said:

I see us doing a great deal more educating of employers. We need to let them know that someone who can't walk isn't necessarily handicapped in regard to employment. Not being able to walk is a disability; a handicap might be something like lack of work experience.

Rehabilitation technology, another new department, was established in 1985, bringing rehabilitation engineering, shop services responsible for fabricating design and building special equipment, and the Courage HANDI-HAM System together under director Bruce Humphrys. It also introduced home modification services, built on experiences gained during the 1960s and 1970s in eliminating architectural barriers from public buildings and private housing. Courage Center launched this service in response to a 1985 survey revealing the need for a comprehensive service to help people make their homes and workplaces more accessible. The service brought together a variety of resources and information regarding building codes, designs, and funding, providing consultation, case management, and follow-up.

With the growth of Courage Center, staff members recognized the need for a unified approach to its educational efforts. The Center had welcomed a steady stream of professional visitors and public tour groups who wanted to observe programs and learn about rehabilitation techniques. In an effort to extend its outreach, staff members had organized several major professional seminars and conferences during the 1970s. Interest was high and the seminars were well attended, but the gymnasium was not adequate for such conferences, and staff members could no longer spare the time to organize them. Courage Center could not continue its educational outreach without addressing these problems.

The Stage III construction in 1986 of an expansive, multipurpose education center solved the space problem. Staffing was taken care of through the establishment in 1988 of Courage Institute, a structure for public and professional outreach, funded by Courage Auxiliary and William Randolph Hearst Foundation.

Courage Center's children's services changed focus, too. Its therapeutic preschool had been established in 1949 at Curative Workshop, and had provided an integrated program of therapy and special services to thousands of children, serving as an important first step for youngsters before they started school. In 1988 new state and federal legislation made public school districts responsible for serving as the lead agencies for the provision of education and therapy services for children from birth to four years. (Schools were already responsible for individuals from 4 to 21 years.) The new legislation resulted in some counties, including Hennepin, discontinuing funding for preschools.

Staff members now faced the challenge of developing new services for multiply-handicapped children. They explored many alternatives and plans involving partnerships with public schools. According to Diane Cross, director of medical rehabilitation, some new programs were already underway by 1989, including the provision of therapy in schools, home-based services in clients' homes, respite care for severely disabled children, a Courage Center day-care program for preschool children, and a pediatric evaluation clinic.

Also initiated in 1989 with a grant from the Walsh Family Foundation of Snowmass, Colorado, were the Courage Lekotek (Swedish for play library) and COMPUPLAY centers. They promote child development and family interaction through a lending library of adapted toys and the use of computer software, addressing the physical and cognitive needs of children with disabilities.

Louis Freeman, here holding Michelle Christopherson of Minneapolis in 1970, has been driving for the therapeutic preschool since 1969.

Andrea Veith of Eden Prairie finds building her language skills with a computer is fun. Joan Waldschmidt, speech and language pathologist, looks on.

Lekotek, modeled after the original center established in Stockholm, Sweden, is the first of its kind in Minnesota. According to Cross:

> Courage Center will continue to offer medically prescribed therapies and related services unavailable through the school districts. We're dedicated to helping children and their families find the resources they need to minimize the impact of disabilities.

FLORENCE STROEBEL KAHN: ONE DOOR OPENS ANOTHER

Flo Kahn had just stopped for a red light that day in 1973. As she waited a car bore down on her, its driver unable to stop. In the impact that followed, Kahn's neck was broken, and from that moment she was quadriplegic. Married and expecting her first child, Kahn had led a full life working as a registered nurse, singing in the Bach Society, playing the piano, and enjoying friends. In an instant she lost her profession and her ability to sing and play the piano, and she lost her child. Later her marriage ended as well. She moved into Courage Residence in 1977 and moved into an apartment with an attendant in March 1979. She discusses the process that took her from loss to acceptance and growth:

Flo Kahn in 1978

When I came to Courage Residence, a big part of me had not been addressed. I had done what I needed to in terms of occupational and physical therapy, but I had not dealt with my feelings, even four years after the accident. We all tend to intellectualize a lot—about our faith and our feelings. And I didn't know how to get myself through grieving.

The counseling my program manager provided helped me learn about feelings. In group therapy, I'd watch people screaming in anger or crying in agony as they tried to deal with loss. As a German-Norwegian, I wasn't going to do that. I was afraid to go to pieces. Still, I was able to learn. My counselor would say, "Just talk about whatever means something to you." So I'd say, "I want to talk about losing my fingers." And he'd help me talk about it and cry about it. Every time I saw him I'd talk about something that I'd lost. Dealing with grief was an important part of adjusting to being disabled.

The first step in grieving is shock—the impact. Most of us have very little recollection of the first few weeks of fighting for life. That numbing is important. The next stage is what I call disruption, when the reality of what you've lost begins to sink in. That's when you get angry and sad, and feel hopeless, anxious, and fearful. The third stage is depression, when you fully realize all you've lost and often stuff feelings inside. The secondary losses are the heavy ones. I couldn't do the gardening, the cooking, make love the same way, or even get out of bed and dress myself—that's when all of it comes home. The fourth stage is recovery, when feelings aren't so intense and you are less self-focused. You begin to see not so much what you've lost as what you can still do. The last stage is growth. You have to work through your grief to get there. Of course, these steps aren't always in order and can weave back and forth.

Volunteering at Courage Center helped me grow. I became a tour guide and one of the groups I gave tours to was the Hennepin Technical School's RN/LPN refresher class. Then the instructor asked me to teach a three-hour segment on rehabilitation and the adjustment process. I still do this regularly. I've also spoken on grieving, loss, and attitude awareness for churches, schools, and other community groups. I've done classes and workshops for St. Olaf College, my alma mater, and other colleges. I've been on the volunteer management and training committee, and I'm a resource for volunteer orientations. As a member of the board of directors at Courage Center, I've served on several committees. You see, one door opens another.

Kahn won many awards for community service, including the YWCA Leadership Award, the Eleven Who Kare award, and in 1987, the St. Olaf Distinguished Alumni Award.

Two other programs, psychosocial services and camping, experienced change and growth in the 1980s. Courage Center had long recognized the importance of serving the emotional and spiritual needs of its clients as well as the physical and vocational. Curative Workshop, forerunner of the Center's medical rehabilitation services, had one clinical social worker, Bob Lepp, who worked primarily with families and children in the therapeutic preschool. With growth came the addition of staff including social workers, psychologists, a neuropsychologist to direct a new community reintegration program for young adults with head injuries, and a chaplain to serve clients and staff at Courage Center and provide a link to their spiritual communities. (Chaplain Barbara Lee is profoundly deaf, giving her a firsthand understanding of people with disabilities.) With a grant from Courage Auxiliary, a psychologist was added in 1988 to work with young men and women living in Courage Residence.

The psychosocial services team provides evaluations, group and individual counseling and therapy, support groups, and a newsletter, *The Meeting Ground,* for families with disabled children.

The camping program also changed as it responded to new needs in the community. Camping director Bob Polland explained:

> In the early years, we appealed to a much broader population, less severely disabled overall. The early camping sessions were largely filled by postpolios. Today we see more people with multiple disabilities, and our programming provides many more options and special programs for campers with diverse needs.
>
> Of our total 20 sessions each year, about half are specialty sessions. We have two oncology sessions for kids with cancer, one for children with burns, a session for metropolitan kids with communication disorders, sports camp, computer camp, amateur radio camp, a leadership camp for deaf teenagers, a session for deaf children, outdoor adventure camp on Winther Island, and others. And we work with more groups and agencies now, including the Minneapolis Public Schools, American Cancer Society, Muscular Dystrophy Association, and Cystic Fibrosis Foundation.

In 1987 Camp Courage undertook a major remodeling effort to update and expand existing facilities.

Another new direction in the 1980s has been the develpment of contractual relationships with other organizations. Courage Center entered into contracts with a growing number of community agencies to provide on-site rehabilitation services. Such agencies include schools, day-care centers, clinics, hospitals, nursing homes, and group homes. One major contract negotiated in January 1989 provides for services to Ebenezer Caroline Center in Minneapolis for clients with head and spinal-cord injuries as well as geriatric clients. Nine new employees help facilitate the program.

Colleen Leitheiser of Sauk Rapids tries her hand at cooking during a 1977 sesstion at Camp Courage.

14 Courage St. Croix

Courage Center entered a new era in October 1988 with the opening of Courage St. Croix, its first satellite facility. At 1460 Curve Crest Boulevard in Stillwater, the center houses an aquatic program and occupational and physical therapy services for people living in the eastern Twin Cities metropolitan area, St. Croix Valley, and western Wisconsin. It also serves as an outreach base for a variety of other Courage programs, including driver education, home modification, rehabilitation engineering, sports and recreation, vocational services, and speech, language, and hearing services.

The concept for Courage St. Croix grew out of discussions between Courage Center board and staff and Katherine (Mrs. Fred C.) Andersen of Bayport. The Andersens had long supported Camp Courage and Courage Center, funding the construction of the Center's pool in 1974. After her husband died in 1979, Katherine Andersen, with the Andersen Foundation and the Bayport Foundation, established the Fred C. Andersen Memorial Fund to endow the pool and aquatics program. As part of Stage III expansion in 1986, the Andersens had also funded a renovation of Courage Center's pool locker, offices, and dressing room areas, making them more accessible and convenient.

Katherine Andersen at Courage St. Croix

Courage Center's successful aquatic and therapy programs led to a decision by Katherine Andersen and her family to help establish similar services in the St. Croix Valley. Courage Center staff conducted a needs survey and initiated a pilot program at Oakland Junior High in Lake Elmo, demonstrating both need and potential support for the proposed facility. Plans began moving forward. Courage Center launched a campaign for $5,875,000 in the fall of 1986—$2,875,000 for capital to build the facility and $3,000,000 for endowment to ensure its continuing operation—in an effort spearheaded by the Andersen, Bayport, Hugh Andersen, and Mahadh foundations. The campaign succeeded, with the help of a $250,000 challenge grant from the Kresge Foundation of Troy, Michigan, and the generous support of the 3M Foundation, the Phipps Foundation, and many other foundations, corporations, and individuals in the St. Croix community and eastern Twin Cities metropolitan area. Construction began in October 1987 and was completed a year later. Peter Polga, who had headed the therapy program at Courage Center since 1976, was appointed director of Courage St. Croix, of which the centerpiece is a large therapeutic swimming pool. The pool is designed for easy access by individuals with disabilities, with wheelchair ramp, built-in whirlpool, roll-out deck, and 92-degree water to soothe muscles and ease pain.

Courage St. Croix signaled a new direction for Courage Center, taking vital services to people in their own communities and drawing from those communities for operational support and endowment funds.

Part Three
A Caring Community

1 A Voluntary Tradition

Courage Center is proud of its voluntary tradition. Its facilities, valued at more than $30 million, have been built almost entirely with gifts from the private sector, and its programs are supported by generous citizens who give time, talent, and dollars. Courage Center programs use third-party payments such as insurance support or government entitlement programs whenever they are available, accounting for 56 percent of its $12.4 million budget in 1988. The other 44 percent comes from grants and gifts of many types from many sectors.

Though it is not possible to list here the thousands of donors and volunteers who have supported Courage Center, each is a vital part of the Courage community. The following groups stand out:
- Volunteers
- Courage Auxiliary
- Boards and committees
- Individual friends and families
- Businesses and corporations
- Foundations
- Social and fraternal clubs and organizations, including Lions, Rotary, Kiwanis, Optimists, American Legion, Veterans of Foreign Wars, Elks, Moose, Eagles, women's organizations, student groups, and schools
- Future Farmers of America and its Corn Drives for Camp Courage
- Pony Express Riders and Courage Wagon Train
- Advertising Federation of Minnesota
- Approximately 1,000 United Ways in a five-state area, accounting for about 8 percent of Courage Center's income
- Guardians of Courage gifts, providing more than $500,000 each year to underwrite programs not supported by fees
- Pillars of Courage, providing endowment or direct support through wills or other forms of estate planning
- Those providing memorial gifts, memberships, and campships, or who give in many different ways

VOLUNTEERS

Volunteers have played a vital role in the Courage Center organization. Volunteers founded the organization in 1928 and worked at Camp Courage and at the network of rehabilitation centers and sheltered workshops established in the 1950s and 1960s. In the mid-1950s, Crippled Child Relief, a group of Twin Cities-area volunteer women, affiliated with the Courage Center organization

Opposite: Campers at a 1978 session at Camp Courage swim in the indoor pool, built with a memorial gift from Harold and Mary Sweatt of Wayzata.

ANDY FULLER: PHOTOGRAPHY IS 90 PERCENT IN THE MIND

Andrew Fuller, a retired bond salesman from Minnetonka, told about his volunteer involvement:

In 1981, a couple of years after retiring, I found I had some time to give as a volunteer. I had sent a little money over the years to Courage Center and received the newsletter, so I decided to drive over and check it out. Mary Wiser knew about a client, Maynard Morken from New Hope, who had difficulty in speaking and was very depressed because of a brain dysfunction—not a stroke, but similar to it. He'd had to retire from his job as a garage mechanic. Maynard had enjoyed photography in the past, and when Mary found out I liked photography too, she jumped on me like a duck on a June bug.

At first Maynard was reticent, but when we talked about photography, he opened up. We got along fine, taking pictures. I was also an assistant for a life enrichment class, and Cindy Raynor, the coordinator, asked me to teach a camera class. I soon decided that to make it permanent we needed a Courage Camera Club. My new assistant was Maynard Morken, delightful to work with. And he has become much more outgoing because of his involvement with the club.

Maynard Morken (left) and Andy Fuller discuss the fine points of photography, in 1983.

The club really took off when volunteer John Miss joined. John was a professional photographer who'd had to retire because of a heart condition. He also had a hearing loss but could read lips very well. John was so helpful and committed. Once when he was in the hospital, his pastor asked, "John, is there anything we can do for you?" John, lying on his back, said, "Well, if there's some money available, we could sure use some cameras in the camera club." So the church donated funds for three self-focusing Minolta Maxxums.

John also saw the need for a device to hold a camera for people in wheelchairs with limited strength in their hands. He devised a "handipod" that clamps onto a wheelchair and is on a bar that can swing out of the way when not needed, and volunteers made some of them. John Miss died in 1987, and we dedicated our new darkroom to him.

We do a lot of things to help our photographers overcome physical limitations—for example, operating a camera with the "sip and puff" method by blowing into a tube to activate the electronic switch or using extension switches on a wheelchair or a talking board. Our members take some fine pictures. I tell them, after all, that photography is 90 percent in the mind and just 10 percent equipment!

for several years to coordinate its direct aid and equipment loan program. The completion of Courage Center in 1973 opened many new opportunities for volunteers, and the number of participants has grown dramatically since then.

By 1987, 6,200 men, women and children were volunteering 56,000 hours annually to help people with disabilities. This included 1,200 individuals working at Courage Center, 174 board and committee members, 520 Courage Auxiliary members, and 4,200 people working throughout the region on local fund-raising projects, on Courage Appeal (a fund drive in areas without united giving), at day camps, and in recreation programs.

Volunteers come from the community, from Courage Auxiliary, and from the clientele of the Center. "The most positive thing that's developed through the years is the way our clients have become important members of the volunteer staff," Mary Wiser, director of volunteer services, said. "Everyone has a gift to give to someone else. Clients have become teachers in life enrichment classes, tour guides, and volunteers in music therapy and many other areas. Some have become board and committee members."

Volunteer Harriet Anderson of Crystal helps Nicole Lambert of Minneapolis explore a toy while Ted Scarlett of Edina gets acquainted with Brittany Williams of New Hope. Volunteer Scarlett repairs and modifies equipment used by young children with disabilities.

The volunteer department has taken a professional approach to placing volunteers, matching up the person with the job, and taking into consideration volunteer as well as client needs. "If you get in the right place and in the right job," Wiser said, "you're going to meet the needs of clients and you're going to be more dependable, enthusiastic, and excited about what you do." Courage Center's mission of helping people with disabilities attracts volunteers, and its creative and varied environment helps volunteers feel right away that they are helping to fulfill that mission. Variety of choice is another factor. This creative approach helped Courage Center's volunteer program win the 1984 Community Service Award of the United Way Voluntary Action Center.

COURAGE AUXILIARY

In 1971 Wilko Schoenbohm invited eight women who had been involved with the Courage Center organization to start a support group to be known as Courage Auxiliary. They accepted the challenge and formed an organization that would become a major donor to Courage Center programs and facilities and a rich resource for volunteer support.

At its first event, a membership brunch in November 1971 at the Governor's Residence (then occupied by Governor Wendell Anderson and his wife, Mary) in St. Paul, more than 100 members signed up. Many were friends of founder June Darling and had worked to help her son, Michael, overcome the effects of cerebral palsy. Courage Auxiliary was officially formed in 1972.

The eight founders served on Courage Auxiliary's first board of directors. From Minneapolis were Marian Champlin, president; Gail Dahlstrom, special events; June Darling, volunteer services; Sara Lieberman, membership; and Mavis Voigt, public relations and education. Pat Haag of Edina was treasurer; directors-at-large were Gray Mackay of Long Lake and Lucille Maun of St. Paul. Other board members were Pat Dunne of Edina, historian; Kay Kromy of Spring Lake Park, recording secretary; Lorene Wendell of Burnsville, corresponding secretary; and directors Dorothy Feinberg of Edina and Irma Wachtler of St. Paul.

Six of the founders of Courage Auxiliary at the Governor's Residence in 1971 are (left to right) June Darling, Marian Champlin, Gail Dahlstrom, Pat Haag, Sara Lieberman, and Mavis Voigt.

In 1972 Courage Auxiliary sponsored its first fund-raising event, a performance of *Summer and Smoke* by the St. Paul Opera Company, gaining widespread publicity for the young organization. Members also planned a week of special activities for the dedication of Courage Center in April 1973 and launched many innovative fund-raising efforts. One, in 1975, gave definition to auxiliary efforts: The Courage Country Fair, held on the transformed Edina farmstead of Pat and Gordon Schuster, raised $32,000. Household and estate sales debuted in 1975 as well, raising $895 from the first effort. Since then, hardworking household and estate sale committee members have raised $145,000 in support of Courage Center programs and facilities.

Auxiliary members took on a new project in 1977 with the sale of a book, *The Best of Helpful Hints,* by Mary Ellen Pinkham, a Courage Auxiliary member. Sales of that and Pinkham's second book raised $71,000. The auxiliary presented project chairs Pat Haag and her sister Janet Warner of Roseville with the Sweetheart Award that has become a traditional way of recognizing outstanding service.

Other projects followed: benefits at the Chanhassen Dinner Theatre, concerts at Orchestra Hall, a used-fur sale initiated in 1981, and the Courage Bridge Classic launched in 1984. In 1982 the Auxiliary organized the Courage Golf Classic, which would become its major annual fund-raising event. The first tournamentt, sponsored by Robert Haag of Edina and Pennzoil, featured Arnold Palmer as guest professional. It raised $58,635. In 1984 Harold Larson of Edina and Harold Chevrolet began sponsoring the annual event, and in 1988 Larson and his wife, Kathryn, became individual sponsors. The Courage Golf Classic has raised more than $850,000 to date, and it contributed substantially to the auxiliary's cumulative total of $1 million in donations to Courage Center in 1985. By the end of 1987 it had given more than $1.5 million.

Courage Auxiliary's fund-raising achievements and volunteer support are vital to the success of Courage Center. Equally important is the goodwill and promotional work done by each of its 500-plus members. The ripple effect of hundreds of dedicated members enlisting friends, associates, and family in the Courage Center cause is beyond measure. The presidents of Courage Auxiliary have been:

1972-73   Marian Champlin, Minneapolis
1973-74   Sara Lieberman, Minneapolis
1974-75   June Darling, Minneapolis/Patricia Haag, Edina
1975-76   Patricia Haag, Edina
1976-78   Jane Houlton, Elk River
1978-79   Jean Wheeler, Edina
1979-80   Lorraine Hasselquist, Minneapolis
1980-81   Jane Houlton
1981-82   Dee Wentworth, Edina
1982-84   Jo Weiner, Edina
1984-86   Mary Oberle, Edina
1986-88   Myrna Abrams, Edina
1988-90   Candy LeGrand, Eden Prairie

PAT HAAG: THE SPIRIT OF COURAGE AUXILIARY

Pat Haag symbolizes the dedication and spirit that has marked Courage Auxiliary since its inception. A founder and first treasurer of the organization, she served as president in 1975-76. Haag chaired the auxiliary's first fund-raiser in 1972 and saw it through many rummage sales, fairs, book projects, and other events. She talked her husband, Bob, into underwriting the first Courage Golf Classic in 1982, ensuring its success. In the summer of 1988 Courage Auxiliary's board of directors pledged $100,000 to a newly established Pat Haag Memorial Endowment Fund, proceeds from which will help clients in the Courage Homecrafters program. Haag was an active volunteer for the program, a craft-oriented vocational service for homebound, disabled artisans. Shortly before her death in March 1988, Haag reminisced:

I became involved with Courage Center through board member Nate Shapiro. I joined the board of Courage Center and served a short time, then I worked with the other founders to start Courage Auxiliary.

We originally worked at the old Franklin and Lyndale location. That building was, I guess, an improvement over previous buildings, although it was hard for me to see that at the time. Wilko was an inspirational, spiritual man, and the other volunteers and staff members were so friendly—I got involved more deeply than I had planned. But it has been fun. We tried anything to raise funds at first. We started small with such large dreams. It's been wonderful to witness our growth and success. Courage Auxiliary is big business now, with about 500 members, but the spirit is still there. I think new members of Courage Auxiliary and new staff members must sense it when they get involved—it's that spirit of Courage.

Harold Larson, sponsor of the Courage Golf Classic, joins committee members after the 1985 tournament. Left to right are Yvonne Makowski of Camp Hill, Pennsylvania, Jane Houlton of Elk River, and Twin Citians Ann Dosch, Mary Oberle, Dorothy Liljegren, Jo Weiner, Twink Larson, and Mary Zicarelli.

HAROLD LARSON: A MORAL OBLIGATION TO HELP PEOPLE

Harold Larson of Edina, former owner of Harold Chevrolet in Bloomington, was born into a family of 15 children near Stanchfield in 1916. When his father died in 1927 and his mother in 1930, the brothers and sisters found themselves facing the Great Depression with no one to turn to but each other.

An older brother purchased a farm near Cambridge, and Larson quit school to join him and three other brothers. He became the "chief cook and bottle-washer" on a dairy farm with no electricity or running water. Larson earned a degree from Macalester College in St. Paul in 1940. He served in the air corps during World War II, then moved to Redwood Falls to work at his older brother Joe's car dealership. In 1955 the brothers opened Larson Brothers Chevrolet in Minneapolis. Two years later Harold opened his own dealership in south Minneapolis, building it into a national sales leader.

Larson learned about Camp Courage from fellow Rotarian Ed Meierbachtol in Le Sueur in 1950 and soon began donating vehicles to the camp. Since then he has provided cars, vans, and trucks and donated many camperships. He sponsors an annual dinner and auction for the Bloomington Rotary Club, with proceeds going to the Rotary Fund for Camp Courage. In 1984, Larson began sponsoring the Courage Golf Classic, a fund-raiser organized by Courage Auxiliary, and he and his wife, Kathryn, are still sponsors.

Harold Larson involves himself in charitable causes such as Courage Center to repay his debt to society: "It's really not too hard to make a living. And after you've done that, you have a moral obligation to help people who need help. That's really the fun of life."

BOARDS AND COMMITTEES

Courage Center's board of directors has the final responsibility for the operation and success of the organization. Its dedication and commitment provide the stability that permits the Center to provide the best possible rehabilitation, independent living, and enrichment programs for people with disabilities. The board, which meets quarterly, has 62 members from across the Upper Midwest and an executive committee of 27 members meeting once a month. Board members each serve on several advisory committees (which also include individuals from the community at large), offering expert counsel to programs at Courage Center. Presidents of the board of directors have been:

1928-30	Dr. Frank Hacking, Minneapolis
1930-32	Carl T. Schuneman, St. Paul
1932-34	Edward M. Conant, Minneapolis
1934-36	Dan I. York, St. Paul
1936-37	James H. Keenan, Minneapolis
1937-38	J. Wallace Maher, Minneapolis
1938-39	John C. Cornelius, Minneapolis
1939-40	Judge Vince Day, Minneapolis
1940-41	Johanna "Jennie" Dowling, Minneapolis
1941-44	Mrs. Alexander Fraser, St. Paul
9/44-12/44	Arthur Geer, Minneapolis
1944-45	Katharine Kohler, Minneapolis
1945-47	May E. Bryne, Minneapolis
1947-49	A. H. Beecher, Minneapolis
1949-52	Frank M. Rarig Jr., St. Paul
1952-53	H. B. Gough, St. Cloud
1953-54	Nobel Shadduck, Annandale
1954-55	Edith McNaughtan, St. Paul
1955-56	Rev. L. Donald Bond, Mankato
1956-57	Emil Cedarholm, St. Paul
1957-60	Rustan O. Thayer, Minneapolis
1960-61	Melvin P. Vollhaber, St. Paul
1961-63	David J. Wick, Albert Lea
1964-65	Dennis W. Dunne, Minneapolis
1965-66	Carroll Elliott, Virginia
1966-69	Edmund C. Meierbachtol, Le Sueur
1969-71	Harry C. Benson, Minneapolis
1971-72	Marvin F. Borgelt, South St. Paul
1972-74	Russell W. Lindquist, Minneapolis
1974-75	Dean B. Randall, Minnetonka
1975-76	Harold C. Mattlin, White Bear Lake
1977-79	Melvin R. Mooty, Minneapolis
1979-80	Corrin H. Hodgson, Rochester
1980-82	Frederick L. Thorson, Minneapolis
1982-84	D. Stephen Farley, St. Paul
1984-86	Donald E. Ryks, Shorewood
1986-88	Alice Mortenson, Edina
1988-89	Robert J. Silverman, Minneapolis

Trustees of the Minnesota Society for Crippled Children and Adults and Camp Courage Foundation meeting in 1963 to reincorporate the foundation are (left to right) Ben Drake Jr., Richard Ordway of St. Paul, Society executive director Wilko B. Schoenbohm, vice-president Herbert Rogers of Maplewood, treasurer R. O. Thayer, president Arthur Rand, Society director of administration Jim Beaton, Ed Meierbachtol, and Tom Snyder of Minneapolis. Not present were members Nobel Shadduck and Jay Phillips.

COURAGE FOUNDATION

As Camp Courage grew and developed and other services were initiated, the need for endowment became ever more urgent. Since Camp Courage was the original facility, efforts to endow that program came first. Benjamin Drake Jr., whose daughter, Priscilla, regularly attended the camp, led in establishing a camp endowment program. Drake and Nobel Shadduck of Annandale, who had played a big part in building the camp, spearheaded the incorporation of Camp Courage Endowment, Inc., in 1959. Four years later, the endowment was expanded and reincorporated to encompass other programs as the Minnesota Society for Crippled Children and Adults and Camp Courage Foundation. The name was shortened to Courage Foundation in 1971.

Courage Foundation encourages additional endowment through special gifts, memorials, and bequests. The foundation, like Courage Auxiliary, is a separate, tax-exempt organization whose investment income is turned over to Courage Center on an annual basis. Its assets reached the $10 million mark in 1988, making it the third largest supporter of Courage Center, following the United Way and Guardians of Courage. Courage Foundation board presidents have been:

1963-70	Arthur Rand Jr., Minneapolis
1970-71	Nobel Shadduck, Annandale
1971-72	Benjamin Drake Jr., Minneapolis
1972-73	Jean McVeety, Minneapolis
1973-76	Nathan Shapiro, Minneapolis
1976-79	Dennis Dunne, Edina
1979-82	James Haverstock, Wayzata
1982-84	E. K. Boberg, Excelsior
1984-86	Donald G. Padilla, Minnetonka
1986-89	Melvin R. Mooty, Edina

2 A Sharing Community

Grants from foundations, contributions from organizations and memorial gifts as well as proceeds from Courage Cards have been vital to the establishment of Courage Center facilities and the development of its services.

FOUNDATIONS

Fifty-three Minnesota-based foundations and six national foundations have provided major grants enabling the construction of Camp Courage, Courage Center, Courage North, the Independent Living Home, and Courage St. Croix. Some foundations such as Kresge Foundation of Troy, Michigan, which has made seven challenge grants, have given many times.

The building of Stage III of Courage Center serves as an example of foundation support. Its fund-raising campaign was launched with a $300,000 challenge grant from McKnight Foundation of St. Paul, matched with grants from Bush Foundation, St. Paul Companies Foundation, Ober (now Mardag) Foundation, and 3M Foundation, all of St. Paul; Pillsbury Foundation, Cargill Foundation, General Mills Foundation, and Gamble-Skogmo Foundation, all of Minneapolis; and Dondelinger Foundation of Brainerd. As the campaign progressed, Kresge Foundation provided an incentive grant of $250,000, and the Kroc Foundation of San Diego helped reach the goal with a $500,000 grant.

FUTURE FARMERS OF AMERICA

One organization whose support goes back more than 35 years is the Minnesota Association of the Future Farmers of America (FFA). In 1954 Lee Asche, advisor of the Freeborn FFA chapter, had an idea for a humanitarian project. He suggested "corn drives" for Camp Courage, which quickly caught on with his agriculture students. They took on the challenge of gleaning corn left by pickers in the field, sold it, and gave the funds to Camp Courage to send children with disabilities to camp. They raised $90, and that summer, a Freeborn resident disabled by polio attended camp with their help.

In 1955 Waino J. Kortesmaki, FFA executive secretary, suggested corn drives as a statewide project, part of the FFA's "Living to Serve" commitment. It was adopted, and high school FFA groups across the state joined in the project. As the years went by, the scope of the drive broadened to include donations from farmers in cash, grain, soybeans, potatoes, and bushels of corn—even pulpwood.

Minnesota FFA members gather corn to benefit Camp Courage, in 1973.

In 1979 the cumulative total contributed by all FFA chapters topped the million-dollar mark, and in the 1988-89 schoolyear the total reached $2 million. The dollars have provided camperships and built facilities vital to the success of camp programs, including a speech therapy building and a greenhouse/horticulture building at Camp Courage and dining hall/activities building at Courage North. The FFA also sponsored a Courage HANDI-HAMS radio training session, underwrote a major film, *Faces of Courage,* and provided funds for a travel camp.

Waino Kortesmaki retired in 1977 after 30 years as executive secretary of the Minnesota FFA. In 1979, when Courage Center presented him with a special service award, he said, "Sometimes we overemphasize making a living. We want to teach these young people to help and cooperate with others. We want to teach them what to do with the heart."

COURAGE WAGON TRAIN

Another group of volunteers has raised funds for Camp Courage each summer with a colorful wagon train. In 1973 Merle Vrieze of Harmony approached members of several saddle clubs and mounted posse groups with an idea. He invited them to join him for a pony express ride to raise funds for children with disabilities at Camp Courage. Twelve riders accepted his invitation, and they made plans to recreate the pony express rides of the Old West by carrying special mail to Camp Courage in relays. In their pouches would be letters written on special stationery by donors, to be mailed from camp. The riders carried out their plans with color and flair, dressing in authentic western garb and picking up donations and pledges along the way. They raised $7,550 for Camp Courage. The idea caught on quickly, and 30 clubs responded to the invitation the following year. By 1976, 500 riders made the trip to Camp Courage, raising $10,000.

The 1987 Wagon Train

The Pony Express Ride of 1978 took a new turn when Darrell Franson of Braham decided to make the trip in a covered wagon and camp along the way. His effort raised about $1,500 through pledges-per-mile, sale of buttons, and solicitation of donations. The next year, Franson and Bob and Ida Paulson of Rochert, near Detroit Lakes, charted an ambitious journey for the wagons—from Fort Francis, Ontario, to Camp Courage, 326 miles. By 1981, word had spread about the adventures of the modern pioneers and their rugged travels, and more people joined the trip. Fourteen wagons and 35 outriders traveled all or part of the 215 miles from Forestville State Park to Camp Courage, raising $7,258, and the Wagon Train kept growing.

The Wagon Train travels about 20 miles a day through heat, dust, wind, and rain, days made lighter by warm welcomes along the route, where as people organize barbecues, picnics, medicine shows, and songfests and give generously to support the cause. "It's a wonderful event run almost 100 percent by volunteers," according to Charles "Chuck" Fullmer, Courage Center's associate executive director of development. At the end of each day the travelers move their wagons into a circle and gather around a campfire to eat, sing, and share stories. The highlight of each trip is the parade into Camp Courage, past rows of admiring and cheering campers. The shouts of welcome and the hugs and kisses wipe out fatigue and stiffness from the long ride, making it all worthwhile.

Since Darrell Franson's solo wagon trek in 1978, the Wagon Train has evolved into a major fund-raiser for Camp Courage. In 1987, 500 people, 300 horses and mules, and 70 wagons participated in a trek from Menominee, Wisconsin, to Camp Courage, a distance of 185 miles. That year, a donation from corporate sponsor Tom Thumb Food Markets, Inc. helped push the cumulative total raised for Camp Courage since 1978 to $400,000. The Pony Express riders still raise funds for camp through special events such as dances, horse shows, and rodeos.

MALCOLM MACKAY JR.: I HAVE MY OWN LIFE TO LIVE

Malcolm Mackay lived in a nursing home for 18 years and worked in a sheltered workshop before living in Courage Residence:

I was really happy to move into the residence where I could be with young people. I got on the Residents' Council and food committee and I learned how to direct an attendant and find an apartment. Now I live in my own apartment, and with Metro Mobility I can get around to Courage Center and ballgames by myself. I work at Courage Center as a volunteer in information and routing. I keep an eye on things—show people where to go—that sort of thing. I love my job: it's the best I've ever had. Courage Center is just like a family—everybody is the same and nobody is sorry for anybody else. I'm glad I now have my own life to live.

Harold Mattlin (left), president of the board in 1975-1976, with Dean Randall, president in 1974-1975.

HAROLD MATTLIN: MY LIFE HAS BEEN ENRICHED

Serving on the boards of both Courage Center and Courage Foundation has been a fulfilling experience. I became involved shortly before taking early retirement in 1973 from the Andersen Corporation, which always set an example for sharing and service. Using some of my energy and experience to create opportunities and services for children and adults who are disabled has added a zest and joy to my life. Each time I go to Courage Center and witness the happy attitudes and courageous daily struggles that many people with disabilities have to achieve greater independence, I leave with the realization that what I have been able to do for Courage Center is outweighed by what participation there does for me. My life has been enriched by the experience.

MEMORIAL GIVING

For many donors, memorials honoring a family member or friend have been a special way of giving. Some examples of creative memorial giving follow.

In 1974 Gail Dahlstrom of Minneapolis, a founder of Courage Auxiliary and dedicated volunteer at Courage Center, and her husband, Donald, wanted to do something that would inspire people who came to Courage Center. They also wanted to commemorate their mothers, Gladys Johnson Idstrom of Edina and Enid Miller Dahlstrom of Balaton. The Dahlstroms commissioned Paul T. Granlund, sculptor-in-residence at Gustavus Adolphus College in St. Peter, to create a bronze sculpture for Courage Center. *The Spirit of Courage,* which was dedicated in April 1975, stands on a patio at the center. Sculptor Granlund explained: "The sculpture portrays a winged figure astride a circle, in a gesture of victorious flight. Three modes of mobility are fused in the work: human, mechanical, and spiritual."

Spirit of Courage

Several other memorial gifts add year-round beauty to Courage Center's lobby and atrium areas. Stage I included a bay area open to the sky where each spring a female mallard laid her eggs and hatched her ducklings safe from predators. The hatching of the eggs was cause for a fiesta for clients and staff, who gathered to watch the parade of the duck family through the dining room and out the door to freedom. Members of the staff gathered the ducklings into a box and held it close to the ground to entice the mother to follow. As they made their way through the maze of people and out the door, cheers resounded through the halls.

Stage III construction added a glass roof over the open area, creating an atrium that extended light to all three floors. The Onan Foundation underwrote the expansion in memory of Robert Onan of Minneapolis. Stage III also included the addition of a glass atrium to the main lobby of Courage Center. Board member Mary Dayton of Long Lake established an endowment fund to purchase and maintain green plants for the entrance, lobby atrium, and dining room atrium, in memory of her parents, Mr. and Mrs. W. W. Haldeman of Minneapolis.

Courage Center atrium

Mary Sweatt and her daughter Martha Reed of Wayzata visited Camp Courage in the early 1960s to see the fragrance garden established and maintained by the Lake Minnetonka Garden Club, of which Reed was a member. It was a cool day in June, and children could not swim in the lake because of the weather. Sweatt learned that some campers seldom or never got to swim during their sessions because of cold or rainy weather, and she decided to do something about it. She talked to her husband, Harold, and agreed to underwrite a new indoor swimming pool at Camp Courage in memory of their son, William R. Sweatt II, who died of polio on a trip to South America. The pool, completed in 1966, became the scene of much fun and joy for hundreds of campers with disabilities.

Clarence and Lucile King of St. Paul played an important part in the development of facilities at Camp Courage and Courage North. After a visit to Camp Courage in 1968, they responded to the need for a recreation center for campers from both campuses, funding the construction of the Judith Ann King Memorial Center, completed in 1970 in memory of their daughter, who was killed in a 1967 car accident. They also established an endowment fund to provide maintenance for the center, which houses a gym, stage, and lounge, and is a hub of activity, hosting wheelchair sports, recreational activities, dramatics, and programs. The recreation center adjoins the Sweatt Memorial pool, creating a recreational complex that serves summer campers and year-round groups using the camp for outdoor educational programs, conferences, and retreats. Lucile King, raised in Staples, also developed an interest in Courage North. She was concerned that, because of the camp's location approximately 200 miles northwest of the Twin Cities, it would be difficult to generate support for it. Upon her death in 1987, she left a generous bequest for the construction of a program center at Courage North, planned for completion in 1989.

When George W. P. Heffelfinger of Deephaven, died in 1970, Courage Center received a substantial sum in memorial gifts restricted to Camp Courage. Because of Heffelfinger's deep interest in nature, these gifts were used to develop a Minnesota Woods project at the camp. The planting of thousands of trees and shrubs indigenous to Minnesota provided a setting for an outdoor nature education laboratory for campers. With significant help from the Minnesota Future Farmers of America, Camp Courage installed surfaced paths enabling people in wheelchairs to utilize and enjoy the woods. In 1987, Heffelfinger's widow, Ruth, funded the remodeling of an existing overlook, creating a year-round nature classroom for campers and school children in the area. Called "Window to the Pond," it serves as headquarters for the camp's naturalist and nature programs.

The Eugene W. Leonard art collection includes work by Gerald Nees of Cory, Indiana.

The Eugene W. Leonard collection of art by disabled artists exhibited in Courage Center's halls was established in 1976 with a special gift from Elizabeth Leonard, Minneapolis, in memory of her husband. The collection includes artwork from around the world, with paintings and drawings by artists who hold a brush in their mouths or use arm or hand braces or other devices. The exhibit, a tribute to the creative spirit in everyone, adds color and beauty as well as inspiration to Courage Center's halls.

When Richard Gunderson of St. Paul retired from the vice-presidency of Hoerner Waldorf, he dedicated himself to community service. One beneficiary was Courage Center, where Gunderson served as vice-president of the board and chairman of both the rehabilitation services and head trauma committees. Soon after Gunderson's death in 1983, his friend, Ben Storey of St. Paul, spearheaded establishment of a memorial fund to be administered by the St. Paul Foundation. Income from the fund is turned over to Courage Center annually in support of programs for individuals with severe head injuries.

COURAGE CARDS

One fund-raising idea that has become a major source of support is Courage Cards. Searching for a new source of funds in 1957, staff members of the Minnesota Society for Crippled Children and Adults asked businesses to consider a donation in lieu of holiday gifts to clients or employees, and they supplied a black-and-white print of a boy on crutches for the companies to send to those on their mailing lists. That idea led to another—printing and mailing holiday letters for businesses in return for a donation to the Society. Then came commercial cards, printed with the name of the company. In 1962 drawings of a child on crutches and of Camp Courage augmented the commercial cards. In 1965 a drawing by disabled artist Grace Sandness of Maple Grove was also offered. In 1970 all these efforts came together with the first all-original-art cards, eight color reproductions of work lent by disabled and able-bodied artists.

Staff member Joyce Vincent and a volunteer committee carried out the project and are still involved today, choosing the verses and art submitted by artists—many of whom have disabilities—from around the nation. Public response to the card program was excellent, and in 1977 the committee named the first honorary chair for the program: Lola Perpich, wife of Minnesota's governor, Rudy Perpich. Others have been Muriel Humphrey (1978), Abigail Van Buren, (1979), Paul Newman and Joanne Woodward (1980), Itzhak Perlman (1981), Patricia Neal (1982), Joni Eareckson Tada (1983), Donny and Marie Osmond (1984), Erma Bombeck (1985), Ted Kennedy Jr. (1986), Eddie Albert (1987), and Ahmad and Phylicia Rashad (1988).

According to Vincent, the Courage Card program supports the Courage Center mission by increasing public awaremess of the artistic talents of persons with disabilities, by enhancing the artists' vocational opportunities, by reaching out to disabled people and the public through the educational message on each card, and by producing significant income for client services through the sale of cards and related products. She said:

> The sending of Courage Cards all over the world helps inform people about Courage Center services. And the fact that artists with disabilities compete with able-bodied artists for the honor of being chosen speaks volumes about their abilities. One key to the success of the program is that people know about and want to help the good work Courage Center does; another is the generosity of the artists.

Actor and racing driver Paul Newman, 1980 honorary Courage Cards chair, swaps racing stories with Chris Olson of Bloomington, who was attending Courage Center's therapeutic preschool.

Princess Margaret of Great Britain admires dolls created by Homecrafter Margaret Bradley while Gina Kugler, director of the program, looks on, in 1974.

3 Special Events and Visitors

Courage Center hosts many special events, including conferences, seminars, and public programs. One of its special traditions is "Christmas Comes to Courage Center," held the weekend before Thanksgiving each year. Staff members and volunteers initiated the holiday festival in 1976 to promote public awareness of Homecrafters products and to thank the artists who donate the use of their art for Courage Cards. They invited musical groups from the community to perform and asked volunteers to bake cookies. The holiday event, an unexpected success, has drawn thousands of visitors each year, bringing together musicians, singers, dancers, clowns, volunteers, and others. Since 1986, the Midwest Chefs Society has created a magnificent brunch for the festivities, open to the public. Income from the sale of tickets to the brunch supports Courage Center programs.

COURAGE CENTER AWARDS

Courage Center has presented several awards each year, both to recognize achievement and to call attention to the needs of individuals with disabilities. The National Courage Award honors individuals who have made a significant contribution on a national or international level to improving services for, or attitudes toward, people with disabilities. Winners receive a bronze replica of the *Spirit of Courage* sculpture at Courage Center.

The national award, sponsored by Rose and Jay Phillips of Minneapolis, evolved from the establishment by the board of the Courage Center Service Award. The first service award was presented in 1978 to Jean Conklin of Bloomington, longtime director of Gillette Children's Hospital in St. Paul and board member of Courage Center. In 1979 the service award went to Waino J. Kortesmaki of New Hope, in recognition of his 30 years of leadership of the Minnesota Association of Future Farmers of America, a group that has raised more than $2 million for Camp Courage. By 1980, when Anne Carlsen received the award, it had been renamed the National Courage Award. A congenital quadruple amputee, she was honored for her work as director of the Anne Carlsen School in Jamestown, North Dakota, and for her efforts to call attention to the need for better opportunities for people with disabilities. She had joined the staff of the Jamestown Crippled Children's School in 1938, when Wilko Schoenbohm was director. The school was renamed in her honor upon her retirement in 1981.

Courage Award winners have also included:
- Max Cleland, Atlanta, former administrator of the Veterans Administration (1981)
- George Conn, Washington, D.C., commissioner of Rehabilitation Services Association (1982)

- Robert and Dorothy DeBolt, Piedmont, California, authors, lecturers, and advocates for the adoption of children with special needs (1983)
- Wilko B. Schoenbohm, Golden Valley, former executive director of Courage Center (1984)
- Joni Eareckson Tada, Woodland Hills, California, author, lecturer, and founder of "Joni and Friends" (1985)
- Itzhak Perlman, violinist (1986)
- Marilyn Price Spivak, Framingham, Massachusetts, cofounder of the National Head Injury Foundation (1987)
- Cliff Crase, Phoenix, editor of *Sports 'n' Spokes* and *Paraplegia News* (1988)

The Rose and Jay Phillips Awards were established in 1964 to call attention to the employment needs and vocational achievements of individuals with disabilities. These awards encourage individuals with disabilities to work toward attaining vocational independence and to promote employment opportunities for men and women with physical limitations.

The Robert A. and Yvonne E. MacDonald Awards, established in 1981, recognize Courage center employees for their outstanding efforts to improve rehabilitation services for children and adults with disabilities. Funding is provided by the MacDonalds, of Edina.

The Melvin R. and Sally Mooty Awards, initiated in 1987 and funded by the Mootys of Edina, provide scholarships for people with disabilities who want to pursue educational goals or gain technical expertise beyond high school.

Outstanding Counselor Awards, funded by the Minnesota Association of Moose, are presented to selected staff members at Camp Courage or Courage North. Originally meant to encourage counselors to seek degrees in rehabilitation, the awards now encourage outstanding counselors to stay in college by augmenting their summer incomes.

THE PHILLIPS LEGACY

In the early 1950s, Jay Phillips of Minneapolis felt he should not continue on the board of directors of the Minnesota Society for Crippled Children and Adults. Although he had a deep personal interest in rehabilitation, intensified by his daughter Helen Phillips Levin's disability from polio, Phillips was distressed that the Society did not seem to be going anywhere. Wilko Schoenbohm, the new executive director, urged Phillips to remain, emphasizing that the organization greatly needed people with his business acumen and deep, abiding concern for people with disabilities. Phillips continued to serve as board member and vice-president for many years and went on to become a trustee of the National Society for Crippled Children and Adults and an early member of Courage Foundation. Currently he serves as an honorary life member of both the Courage Center and Courage Foundation boards.

In 1964 Jay Phillips and his wife, Rose, established the annual Rose and Jay Phillips Awards to recognize vocational achievements of people with disabilities, and in 1980 they began funding the annual National Courage Award, presented to individuals in recognition of exceptional contributions to rehabilitation. Each year, Courage Center presents the Phillips awards to five men and women who have achieved success in their vocations despite physical disabilities. Winners receive a plaque and a $500 award.

VISITORS

Courage Center has attracted visitors from around the world since its opening in 1973. People come to observe, to participate, and to learn. Others come as part of special events or programs. Some come for help in building rehabilitation programs and facilities of their own.

LADY HANNAH MOMOH, wife of Major General Dr. J. S. Momoh, president of Sierra Leone, Africa, at Courage Center in 1986. She sought information and guidance in building a training center for children with disabilities. Board president Alice Mortenson accompanied her on a tour.

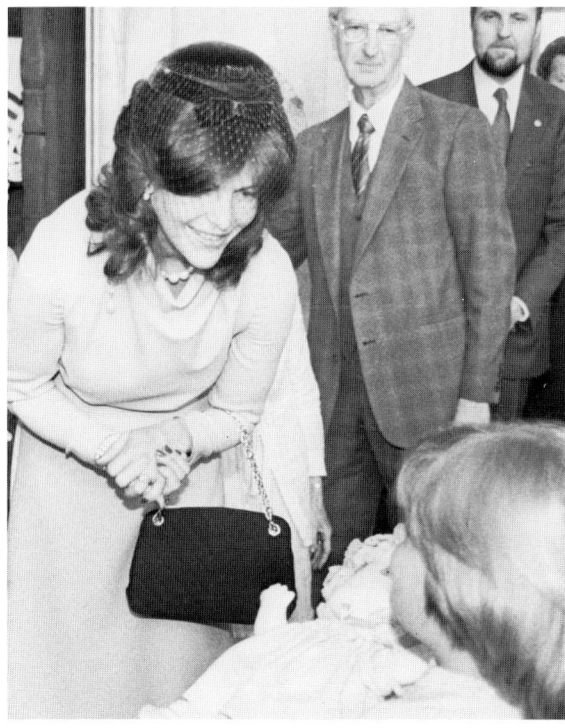

QUEEN SILVIA OF SWEDEN greets Courage Girl of the Year Julie Trebtoske of Minneapolis while visiting Courage Center in 1982 as part of Scandinavia Today, a Minnesota festival. Queen Silvia is active in programs for people with disabilities in her home country.

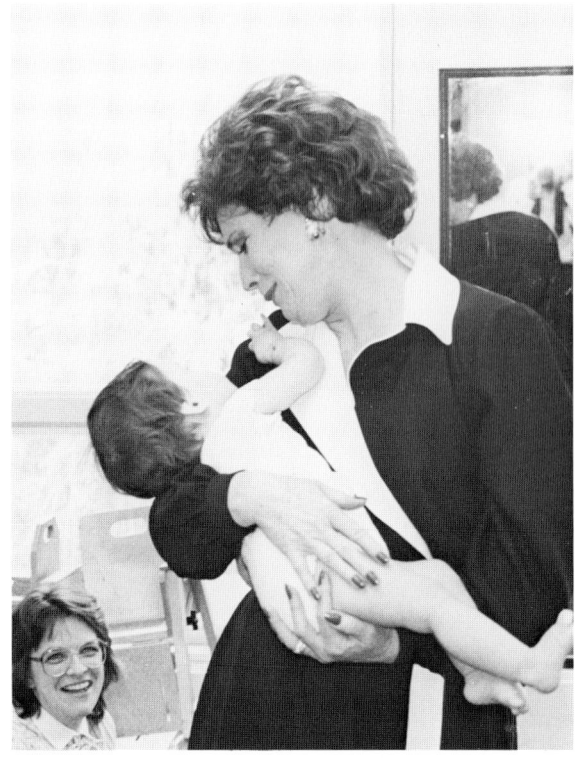

*JEHAN SADAT,
widow of Egyptian president
Anwar Sadat, at Courage Center
in 1983. She later wrote:
"I have visited many
rehabilitation centers around the
world, and I can confidently say
that Courage stands out as the
most impressive, comprehensive
facility I have ever seen."*

*PRINCE HENRI and
PRINCESS MARIA THERESA
OF LUXEMBOURG
gather information at Courage
Center for a foundation working
with people with disabilities
in their country, in 1984.
Attending a sports demonstration
are (left to right)
tour guide Betty Held,
executive director David Hersey,
Prince Henri,
Courage Foundation president
Don Padilla,
Princess Maria Theresa,
and director of sports, physical
education and recreation
Bob Szyman.
Prince Henri played basketball
from a wheelchair
before joining the tour.*

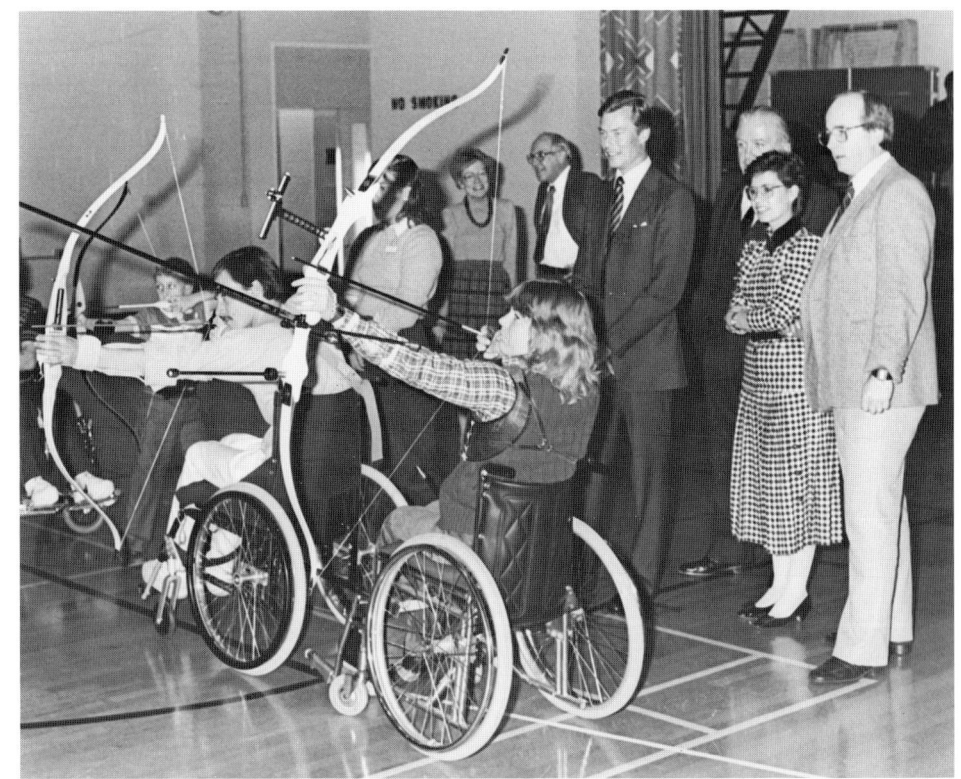

KEVIN SULLIVAN: THE SPIRIT OF ST. LOUIS

Kevin Sullivan of St. Louis Park met Reeve Lindbergh Brown when he was asked to be the volunteer tour guide during her visit to Courage Center. Brown, youngest daughter of aviator Charles A. Lindbergh and Anne Morrow Lindbergh, had come to Courage Center to see what was being done for children with severe disabilities. Her son, Jonathan Lindbergh Brown, had recently died of spinal meningitis and encephalitis, and she had established an award in his name within the Charles A. Lindbergh Fund.

Sullivan was living at Courage Residence, gaining independent living skills after recuperating from a diving accident in which he broke his neck. He told Brown, "I would like to be the first quadriplegic to fly across the Atlantic." Everyone laughed, he said later, except Brown. She queried him about his goal, learning that he had been a commercial pilot and, at the time of the accident, a student in aeronautical studies at the University of North Dakota.

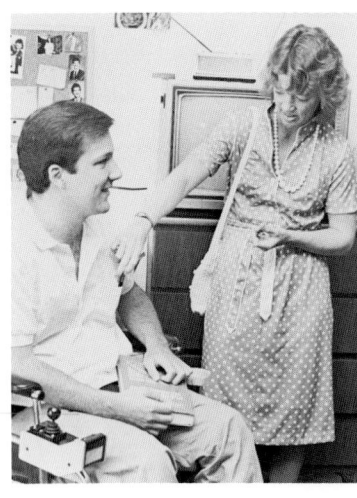

Reeve Lindbergh Brown autographs a book on flying for tour guide Kevin Sullivan during her visit to Courage Center in 1985.

Sullivan became the first recipient of the Jonathan Lindbergh Brown Award of $10,580—the cost of Lindbergh's original Spirit of St. Louis. Sullivan used the award money to purchase a van with hand controls and a special computer to help him with his studies. He learned to drive at Courage Center and finished his degree at the University of Minnesota: "I was looking around for employment and got a job at Flying Cloud Airport at a flight school. They offered me a job opening up and managing a flight school in La Crosse, Wisconsin. So I spent a little over a year there and successfully managed the business, and we sold it to another flight school. Then they asked me to come back up here and run the flight school at Flying Cloud Aviation in Minneapolis."

Sullivan has flown a few times since the accident: "I got in a plane and took off and landed by myself, but once I get on the ground I have to have someone next to me who can steer the plane with his feet. I have looked into planes that are accessible for handicapped people—an organization in California offers equipment for disabled people who want to operate planes. I still have my dream of crossing the Atlantic!"

According to executive director David Phillips, "Courage Center will push to continue to expand the involvement of many people in the organization. We're in the business of providing the opportunity for people to discover the joy of serving human need."

Let us confess, with great humility, that through the providences of God, the historic achievement of Western man has been to do something not simply for himself but for mankind as a whole—something so big that our own parochial history is going to be swallowed up by the results of it. By making history we have transcended our own history . . . To be allowed to fulfill oneself is a glorious privilege for any of God's creatures.

ARNOLD J. TOYNBEE, *Civilization on Trial*

4 Looking Ahead

"The future of Courage Center," says David Phillips, executive director, "will come by direction of the board of directors." The formal planning process is in place, building on the guidelines defined under former executive director David Hersey in 1984, with the planning committee presenting updated plans to the board each year.

Strategic objectives will be tied to expanding Courage Center's mission to help people with disabilities achieve independence, productivity, and integration into all of society, according to Phillips: "We will seek to meet and exceed the public's expectation of a human service agency, and we will seek to do the same for our clients." To keep a clear focus on providing quality services to clients, the marketing program, under the direction of Jim Thalhuber, associate executive director of marketing and public relations, will play an increasingly important role in identifying needs in order to design programs to meet those needs.

Changing human needs will affect future programs of Courage Center. As Americans get older, disabilities associated with age, such as stroke, arthritis, cognitive disorders, and vision and hearing impairments, will increase, and services will address those disabilities. In addition, Phillips says, "The use of technology in rehabilitation to increase communication, mobility, and independent living will dramatically affect opportunities for people with disabilities, and Courage Center will be there to help give leadership."

Geographic expansion is in Courage Center's future, too. The new Courage St. Croix facility in Stillwater may be a forerunner of facilities in other communities. The national Courage Stroke Network is already taking the presence of Courage Center into every state, and individuals from all over the country are coming to Courage Residence. One program, the Courage HANDI-HAM System is international in scope, and a growing number of interns from other countries is accepted for training at Courage Center.

The accomplishments are great, but the work is not done. Where there is need, that need will continue to be addressed. Where barriers remain, they will be removed. Sharing the vision of its founders, gathering strength from each other, the community of Courage will go on working for a better life for everyone. As Courage Center moves into its next decade, David Phillips looks back with gratitude on its first 60 years. He quotes a prayer from Dag Hammerskjold former secretary general of the United Nations: "For all that has been, 'Thanks!' For all that will be, 'Yes!' "

Index

Page numbers in italics indicate illustrations of listed subjects.

Ability Building Center (ABC) (Rochester, MN), 24-25
Abrams, Myrna, 89
Adamson, Margaret, 42
Advertising Federation of Minnesota, 85
Albert, Eddie, 99
Allen, Edgar F. "Daddy," 9-10
Allen, Homer, 9
Altman, Brian, *26*
American Cancer Society, 82
American Legion, 85
American Medical Association. Council on Physical Medicine and Rehabilitation, 21
American Physical Therapist Association, 13
American Red Cross, 60
Amherst H. Wilder Charity (St. Paul, MN), 21
Andersen Foundation, 51, 60, 83
Andersen, Fred C., 51
Andersen, Katherine [Mrs. Fred C.], 51, *83*
Anderson, Gov. C. Elmer, *28*
Anderson, Harriet, *87*
Anderson, Margaret, 51, *64*, 73
Anderson, Mary [Mrs. Wendell], *87*
Anderson, Michael, *62*
Anderson, Gov. Wendell, *87*
Anne Carlsen School (Jamestown, ND), 22, 101
Architectural barriers committee, 35
Asche, Lee, 93
Aune, Olga, *43*

Baker Foundation, xi, 28
Barden-LaFollette Act (1943), 21
Barnes, Kate [Mrs. Arthur], 9
Baron, Joan [Mrs. Tony], 77
Baron, Lisa, 77
Baron, Tony, 77
Bateman, Dr. Ronald, *58*
Bauman, Carl, 24-25
Baustian, Dan, *52*
Bayport Foundation, 51, 60, 83
Beaton, James, 49-50, 76, *92*
Bedhauer, Kaye, *51*
Beecher, A. H., 91
Bellows, Howard, 36
Benson, Harry C., 91
Bergey, Alyce, *65*
Berglund, Lee, 51
Berquam, June [Mrs. Warren], 61
Berquam, Warren, 61

Best of Helpful Hints, The (M. E. Pinkham), 88
Boberg, E. K., 92
Bobleter, Kevin, *48*
Bombeck, Erma, 99
Bond, Donald, Jr., *48*
Bond, Rev. L. Donald, *48*, 91
Booth, Robert, 21
Bordewich, Harald, 17
Borgelt, Marvin F., 91
Boyle, Michelle, *58*
Bradley, Margaret, *43, 48, 100*
Brown, Jonathan Lindbergh, 105
Brown, Reeve Lindbergh, *105*
Bryne, Mary E., 91
Bunge, Benjamin, 49-50
Bunge, Christian, Jr., 49
Bunge, Mrs. Christian, Jr., 49
Burke, Amy, *7*
Burke, Bruce, *7*
Burke, Cathy [Mrs. Bruce], *7*
Burke, Debbie, *7*
Bush Foundation, 69, 79, 93
Bush Loan Fund, 79

Camp Courage (*See also* Courage North), 6, 24, 35, 39-40; cabins, *28;* campers, 7, *29-30, 32, 43, 77, 84;* chapel- amphitheater, 30; cookouts, *3;* dedication, 30; design, 27; expansion, 31, 33; facilities, *3, 28;* fire, 33; fragrance garden, *31;* funding and fund-raising, 27 28, 30, 93-94, 95-96, 98; groundbreaking, *28;* H. B. Gough and, 27; Humphrey Island site, 34; infirmary, 29; Judith Ann King Recreation Center, 33, 97; L. Marzinske on, 75; E. Meierbachtol and, 40; H. G. Metcalf and, 27; *Minneapolis Tribune* on campers, 31-32; Minnesota Woods project, 98; Moose Association and, 34; name, 27; nature building, 30; Outstanding Counselor Awards, 102; overnights, *23;* B. Polland on, 82; pool, 82, *84,* 97-98; programs, 82; radio camp, 44; F. Rarig and, 27; B. Russ on, 36-37; G. Schlenk and, 27; W. Schoenbohm and, *28;* N. Shadduck and, 27; site, 27, 33; speech and hearing program, *3, 30, 32, 34;* staff, *18, 26;* therapy, 31; M. P. Vollhaber on, 34; volunteers, 85; J. Voss on, 29; R. I. Wachtler and, 27
Camp Courage Endowment, Inc., 92

Camp Courage Foundation (*See also* Courage Foundation), 92
Camp Kiwanis (Marine on St. Croix, MN), 7, 18-20, 27; campers, 7, *19-20;* speech and hearing programs, 18, 20, 32; staff, *18;* M. Thompson on, 20
Camp Winnebago, 49
Cargill Foundation, 93
Carlsen, Anne, 101
Carleton College (Northfield, MN), 11
Carman, Ned, *44*
Carstens, Jill, 50
Casey Albert T. O'Neil Foundation, xi
Casper-Robeson, Karen, *47*
Cavanaugh, Joe, *38*
Cedarholm, Emil, 91
Cedar Valley Rehabilitation Center (Austin, MN), 24
Champlin, Marian, *87-88*, 89
Charles A. Lindbergh Fund, 105
Charles, Marian, *29*
Chatterton, Carl C., 9
Chippewa Valley Wheelers, 47
Christ, Konnie, *33*
Christiansen, Cindy, 67
Christiansen, Mycah, 67
Christopherson, Michelle, *80*
City of Minneapolis Award, 23
Civilian Conservation Corps, 18
Cleland, Max, 101
Coffield, Leslee, *36*
Colvin, Gail, 68
Community Chest (*See also* United Fund), 38, 42
Conant, Edward M., 91
Conklin, Jean, 42, 68, 101
Conn, George, 101
Conroy, Carolyn, 17
Control Data Corporation, 70
Cornelius, John C., 91
Courage Auxiliary, 55, 68, 82, 92; board of directors, 87, 112; founding, 87; fund-raising activities, 78, 80, 88; P. Haag on, 89; presidents, 89; Sweetheart Award, 88
Courage Cards, 23, 98-99
Courage Center (*See also* Camp Courage; Courage North; Courage St. Croix; Curative Workshop; Minnesota Association for Crippled Children; Minnesota Association for Crippled Children and Adults, Inc; Minnesota Conference for the Disabled; Minnesota Society for Crippled

Courage Center *(continued)*
Children and Adults, Inc.), 2, 55; and handicapped access, influence, 35; aquatic programs, 51, 60-61, *63,* 83; art therapy program, 67; atmosphere, 1; atrium, *97;* awards, 101-102; board of directors, 91; brain injury program, 57; budget, 51, 85; camping (*See also* names of camps), 1-2, 6; children's services, 80-81; C. Christiansen on, 67; "Christmas Comes to Courage Center," 101; G. Colvin on, 68; COMPUPLAY Centers, 80; computers and, 70, 80; contractual relationships, 82; Courage Appeal, 87; Courage Camera Club, 86; Courage Center Service Award, 101; Courage Classroom, 65; Courage Lekotek, 80-81; *Courage News,* 68; Courage Song, 73; Cub Scouts, *62-63;* dedication, 88; donors, 85; disabled, role in, 1; driver education, 6, *68-69;* C. Duff on, 57; education and outreach services, 58, 80; endowment appeal, 73; expansion, 57-60; facilities, 2-3; five-year objectives, 75-76, 78; funding and fund-raising, 49-51, 66, 70, 76, 78-79, 83, 85-90, 93-94, 95-99; foundations and, 93, 97; R. E. Fulford on, 69; future of, 106-107; Future Farmers of America and, *93-94;* giftshop, 43; golden anniversary, 73; groundbreaking, *48,* 50; Guardians of Courage, 51, 85, 92; hearing impaired programs, 62; V. C. Heath on, ix; D. Hersey and, *74-76*, Independent Living Home, 73, 93; leadership, change in, 73-74; E. W. Leonard art collection, 98; J. Leske on, 71; life enrichment classes, 65-67; lobby, *2;* M. Mackay Jr. on, 96; F. Madden on, 75-76; L. Marzinske on, 75; H. Mattlin on, *96;* medical rehabilitation and education, 2, 5, 41, 57-58; Melvin R. and Sally Mooty Awards, 102; memorials, 97-98; mission statement, 75; M. Moilanen on, 68; music therapy program, *66-67;* name change, 73; National Courage Award, 101-102; D. Nelson on, 68-69; J. Olson and, 68; origins, 1, 9;

108

Courage Center *(continued)*
outreach programs, 6; D. A. Phillips and, *76-78*, 106-107; Pillars of Courage, 85; pool, 2, 51, 60, 83; psychosocial services, 82; C. Raynor on, 65-67; rehabilitation centers, volunteers, 85; rehabilitation engineering program, 69-71; rehabilitation technology department, 6, 70, 80; Robert A. and Yvonne E. MacDonald Award, 102; Rose and Jay Phillips Award, 101-102; Saturday Club, 61; sculpture, *97;* services, 1-2, 5-6, 51, 57, 62; sheltered workshops, volunteers, 85; site, 50; special events, 101; sports, physical education and recreation programs (*See also* Rolling Gophers, Rolling Rascals, Rolling Rowdies), 5, 61-63; staff, *60-61, 75;* technological work evaluation program, 70; Teen Club, 61; J. B. Vickerman on, 60-61; J. Vincent on, 23, 99; visitors, *103-104;* vocational services, 5-6, 78-79; volunteers, 6, 85-*86,* 87, 89; W. B. Schoenbohm on, xi, 74; R. Szyman on, 63; M. Wirth-Davis on, 79-80

Courage Center Duluth Area Services, 62

Courage Foundation, 50, 102; board members, *96;* presidents, 92; W. Schoenbohm and, 73-74

Courage HANDI-HAM System, 6, 80, 102; funding, 44, 94; N. Carman and, *44;* M. Pranghofer on, *45;* radio camp, *44;* services, 44-45; staff, 44; West Coast session, 44

Courage Homecrafters, 15, *42,* 78-79, *100;* funding, 89; Minnesota Homecrafters and, 43

Courage Home Enterprises, 79

Courage Institute, 6, 78, 80

Courage North, 6, 97; campers, *56;* expansion, 56; facilities, *4;* funding, 93, 98; hearing-impaired program, 55-56; Out-standing Counselor Awards, 102; R. Polland on, 55; programs, *4,* 56; radio camp, 44; site, donated, 55

Courage Pony Express Riders, 85, 95-96

Courage Residence, 6-7, 78, 102; M. Anderson and, 51, *64;* atmosphere, 52 53; dedication, 53; expansion, 78; M. Moilanen on, 53; J. Olson and, 51; planning, 51; residents, *52-53*

Courage Rolling Gophers, *46-47,* 62, 63

Courage Rolling Rascals, *62*

Courage Rolling Rowdies, 62

Courage St. Croix, 107; facilities, *4;* funding, 83; opening, 83; pool, 83; programs, *4*

Courage Stroke Club. *See* Courage Stroke Network

Courage Stroke Network, *5*-6, 67, 102; expansion, 68; J. Karon on, *67;* origins, 67; services, 68; staff, 25; *Stroke Connection,* 68

Crase, Cliff, 102

Courage Wagon Train, 85, 94-95

Crippled Child Relief, 85, 87

Cross, Diane, 42, 80-81

Cunningham, Glenn, *28*

Curative Workshop (*See also* Courage Center), 7, *41;* cerebral palsy preschool, 22, 42, 77, 80; established, 13; funding, 42; mergers, *41-44,* 46-47; move to Courage Center, 41; occupational therapy, *15;* physical therapy, 13; services, *14,* 41-42, 58; volunteers, *14*

Cystic Fibrosis Foundation, 82

Dahlstrom, Donald, 97
Dahlstrom, Enid Miller, 97
Dahlstrom, Gail, 87-*88,* 97
Darling, June [Mrs. Andrew], 78, 87-*88,* 89
Darling, Michael, 87
Day, Judge Vince, 91
Day camp, 6, 39
Dayton, Mary, 97
DeBolt, Dorothy, 102
DeBolt, Robert, 102
DeParcq, William H., xi
Depression (1930s), 13
Des Moines Road Runners, 46
Deubener, Lydia [Mrs. Walter], 56; and Courage North, 55
Deubener, Walter, 56; and Courage North, 55
Disabled American Veterans, 46
Disabled persons (*See also* Disabled children); affirmative action and, 54; architectural barriers, 2, 35, 82; attitudes toward, 1-2, 10, 13, 35, 53 54; employment, 15; law and legislation, 15, 21, 54, 80; personal narratives, 7, 11; role in society, 1-2; transportation, *12,* 14, 36; types of disabilities, change in, 57; veterans, 13, 21; vocational training, 15; WWII and, 21
Disabled children: conferences about, 9; education, 7, *12-15,* 80-81; policy of state, 9; programs for, 9-10
Division of Vocational Rehabilitation, 42
Dondelinger Foundation, 93
Donnelly, Pat, *38*
Dosch, Ann, *90*
Dowling, Dorothy, 17
Dowling, Johanna "Jennie" (Bordewich) [Mrs. Michael J.], 10, *17*-18, 91

Dowling, Kathleen B., 17
Dowling, Marjorie, 17
Dowling, Michael J., *11,* 17
Drake, Benjamin, Jr., 92
Drake, Priscilla, 92
Dressen, Lindsay, *59*
DuBois, George, *42*
Duepner, Linda, *38*
Duff, Chris, 57
Duluth (MN): disabled persons, programs for, 9, 15; occupational therapy programs, 15
Duluth Association for the Physically Handicapped, 15
Duluth Crippled Children's Committee, 15
Duluth Junior League, 22
Duluth Rehabilitation Center, 15, 24
Dunne, Dennis W., 91-92
Dunne, Pat, 87

Eagles (order), 85
Easter Seals, 15
Eavis, Lori, *32*
Ebenezer Caroline Center (Minneapolis, MN), 82
Eichorn, Richard, 44
Eisenhower, Julie (Nixon), *50*
Eleven Who Kare award, 81
Elks, Order of, 85
Ellerbe Architects, 27
Ellerbe, Thomas, 27
Elliott, Carroll, 91
Englin, Charles F., *12*
Eugene W. Leonard Art Collection, 98

Faces of Courage (movie), 94
Farley, D. Stephen, 91; on W. Schoenbohm, 73-74
Farmer's Holiday Association, 13
Federal Rehabilitation Services Administration, 70
Feinberg, Dorothy, 87
Felt, Christopher, *3*
Felt, Jody, *3*
Fogarty, Mimi [Mrs. Tom], 56
Fogarty, Tom, 56
Foss, Cheryl, *30*
Foss, Gov. Joe, *30*
Franciscan International Award, 74
Franson, Darrell, 95-96
Fraser, Mrs. Alexander, 91
Fred C. Andersen Memorial Fund, 83
Freeman, Louis, *80*
Fulford, Ray E., 69
Fuller, Andrew, *86*
Fullmer, Charles "Chuck," 95-96
Future Farmers of America, 93, 101; and Courage Center, 85, 93-*94*

Gabrielson, Harold R., 21
Gamble-Skogmo Foundation, 93
Geer, Arthur, 17, 91
Geer, Marie [Mrs. Arthur], 17
General Mills Foundation, 93
Gillette, Arthur, 9

Gillette Children's Hospital, 7, 9
Golden Valley Health Center, 78
Goad, Michael, *50*
Gough, Harry B., 17, 91
Governor's Relief Committee, 17
Granlund, Paul T., 97
Griffith, Ann, 49
Grimm, Mary, *71*

Haag, Pat, 87-*88, 89*
Haag, Robert, 88-89
Haarstick, Maxine [Mrs. Wallace], 67
Haarstick, Wallace, 67
Hacking, Dr. Frank, 10, 91
Hagel, Sue, *62*
Haldeman, Mr. and Mrs. W. W., 97
Haley, Elvin, *65*
Halker, Carl, *34*
Halker, Heidi, *34*
Halker, Marilyn [Mrs. Carl], 34
Halker, Nils, *15*
Hammerskjold, Dag, 107
Harmon, Margaret [Mrs. Reuel], 44
Harold Chevrolet, 88, 90
Haskins, James, 53-54
Hasselquist, Lorraine, 89
Haverstock, Henry, Jr., *35-36*
Haverstock, James, 92
Head, Jaime, *39*
Head of the Rapids Camp, 18
Healy, Phyllis Rodrick, 42, 51
Heath, Vernon C., *ix,* xi
Hedberg, Dan, *70*
Heffelfinger, George W. P., 98
Heffelfinger, Ruth [Mrs. George W. P.], 98
Held, Betty, *50, 104*
Henri, Prince of Luxembourg, *104*
Hersey, David, *74-76, 104*
Hite, Barry, 53
Hodgson, Corrin H., 91
Hoffman, Harvey, 62
Hollern, Mrs. and Mrs. John, xi
Honeywell, 69
Houlton, Jane [Mrs. Kendall], 39-40, 89-90
Houston County Historical Society (MN), 49
Hovick, Larry, 27
Hugh Andersen Foundation, 83
Hull, Minnie, 31
Humphrey, Sen. Hubert H., *32,* 34
Humphrey, Muriel [Mrs. Hubert H.], 34, 99
Humphrey, Ronald, *32*
Humphrys, Bruce, 44, 80

Idstrom, Gladys Johnson, 97
Ingold, Mary Beth, *59*
International Year of the Disabled, 73
Iowa State Hospital School (Iowa City, IA), 22
Iron Range Rehabilitation Center (Virginia, MN), 24

Jambeck, Toivo "Toy," 18, 29
Jensen, Ward, 44
Johnson, Bridgett, 77
Jonathan Lindbergh Brown Award, 105
Jones, Dorothy, 12
Josephs, Elmer, 18
Judith Ann King Recreation Center (Camp Courage), 33, 97-98
Junior League, 42

Kahn, Florence Stroebel, 81
Karon, Justin, 67
Kasell, Pat, 68
Kate Barnes classes for crippled children, 15
Keenan, James H., 91
Kennedy, Ted, Jr., 99
Kenney, Molly, 4
Kenning, Pearl, 15
Kenny, Sister Elizabeth, 35
Kiewel, Harold, 29
King, Clarence, 33, 97
King, Lucile [Mrs. Clarence], 33, 97-98
Kiwanis Clubs, 85
Klawitter, Joseph R., 39
Klitzke, Deborah, 33
Knorr, Beverly, 33
Kohler, Katharine, 91
Kortesmaki, Waino J., 93-94, 101
Kottke, Dr. Frederic J., 21
Kresge Foundation, 83, 93
Kroc Foundation, 93
Kromy, Kay, 87
Krusen, Dr. Frank, 21-22, 25
Kugler, Gina, 100
Kulick, Marcia Bevard, 60, 63
Kusske, Margaret, 8-9

Lake Minnetonka Garden Club, 97
Lake Region Sheltered Workshop (Fergus Falls, MN), 24
Lambert, Nicole, 87
Lampert, Robin, 63
Lance, Hal, 79
Larkin, Arthur, 12
Larson, Harold, 88, 90
Larson, Kathryn [Mrs. Harold], 88, 90
Larson, Twink, 90
Lawrence, Marjorie, 30
Lebahn, Casey, 61
Lebahn, Jason, 61
Lebahn, Terry [Mrs. Tony], 61
Lebahn, Tony, 61
Lee, Barbara, 82
LeGrand, Candy, 89
Lehman, Louis, 16
Lehmann Center, 7
Leitheiser, Colleen, 82
Leonard, Elizabeth [Mrs. Eugene W.], 98
Lepp, Robert F., 67, 82
Leslie, Jonathan, 71-72
Levin, Helen Phillips, 102
Lindbergh, Anne Morrow [Mrs. Charles A.], 105
Lindbergh, Charles A., 105
Lieberman, Sara, 87-88, 89

Liljegren, Dorothy, 90
Lindquist, C., 21
Lindquist, Russell W., 91
Lions Club, 85
Ljungren, LeRoy, 45
Lloyd, Scotty, 66
Lone Craftsman program. See Minnesota Association for Crippled Children
Lohmann, Irene "Willie," 25
Lovering, Robert, 37
Lowry, Elizabeth [Mrs. George], 25

MacDonald, Robert A., 102
MacDonald, Yvonne E., 102
McGerr, Linda, 8-9
McGrane, Debby, 29
Mackay, Gray [Mrs. Malcolm], 37-38, 43, 87
Mackay, Malcolm, Jr., 96
Mackay, Malcolm, Sr., 37-38
McKnight Foundation, 93
McNaughtan, Edith, 91
McPeek, Lorena, 14
McVeety, Jean, 92
Madden, Frank, 75
Mahadh Foundation, 83
Maher, J. Wallace, 91
Makowski, Yvonne, 90
Mankato Rehabilitation Center, 24, 67
Marblehead Sanatorium (Boston, MA), 15
Mardag Foundation, 93
Margaret, Princess, 100
Maria Theresa, Princess of Luxembourg, 104
Marsh, Bonnie, xii, 1
Martin, Mary, 32
Marzinske, Linda, 75
Mattlin, Harold C., 91, 96
Mauer, Don, 69
Maun, Lucille, 43, 87
Mayo Clinic (Rochester, MN), 13, 17, 21
Meierbachtol, Edmund C., 41, 90-92; and Camp Courage, 32, 40; J. Houlton on, 40
Metcalf, H. G., 27
Metro Mobility, 36
Metropolitan Community College, 7
Michael Dowling School, 7, 9
Michael Dowling Urban Environmental Learning Center, 26
Midnite Squares, 61
Midwest Chefs Society, 101
Miller, Chad, 5
Minneapolis Junior League, 22
Minneapolis Literacy Program, 23
Minneapolis Public Schools, 82
Minneapolis Rehabilitation Center, 24
Minneapolis Rotary Club: Service Above Self Award, 74
Minneapolis Tribune: on Camp Courage campers, 31-32
Minneapolis YWCA, 23
Minneapolis Zonta Club, 23

Minnesota: Depression (1930s), 13; disabled children, education, 9, 12-14; disabled persons, law and legislation, 15
Minnesota. Bureau of Services for Crippled Children, 15-16
Minnesota. Department of Education, Special Education Division, 15
Minnesota. Department of Re-education, 13
Minnesota. State Council on Disability, 36
Minnesota Amateur Sports Commission, 63
Minnesota Association for Crippled Children (*See also* Courage Center; Minnesota Association for Crippled Children and Adults, Inc; Minnesota Conference for the Disabled; Minnesota Society for Crippled Children and Adults, Inc.), xi; affiliation, National Society for Crippled Children and Adults, 15; brochures, 10; Depression (1930s) and, 13; direct aid program, 15-16; disabled children, education, 13-15; funding and fund-raising, 15, 42; goals, 10, 13; incorporated, 10; Lone Craftsmen (*See also* Courage Homecrafters), 15, 42, 78; name change, 21; orthopedic clinics, 15; services, 16
Minnesota Association for Crippled Children and Adults, Inc.: camping programs, 17-20; direct aid, 21; directors, 21; J. Dowling and, 18; established, 21; hearing and speech programs, 20-21; name change, 21; services, 20-21; WWII years, 21
Minnesota Conference for the Disabled, 9-10
Minnesota Council for Special Education, 23
Minnesota Future Farmers of America, 32-33, 93-94
Minnesota Handicapped Skiers Association, 47
Minnesota Handi-Hams (See also Courage HANDI-HAM system): merger, 44
Minnesota Homecrafters: funding, 43; giftshops, 43; mergers, 42-43; move to Courage Center, 43; program, expansion, 42; volunteers, 43
Minnesota Public Health Association, 15
Minnesota Society for Crippled Children and Adults, Inc. (*See also* Duluth Rehabilitation Center), xi, 92; and Camp Courage Foundation, 92; and Courage Cards, 98;

Minnesota Society for Crippled Children and Adults, Inc. *(continued)* and National Society for Crippled Children and Adults, 38; and St. Paul Rehabilitation Center, 21-22; aquatic programs, 60; architectural barriers and, 35-36; camping (*See also* Camp Courage), 39; community services staff, 39-40; development committee, 22; development fund, 23; funding and fund-raising, 22-23, 27-28, 30, 37-39, 49-50; headquarters, 37-38; mergers, 41-44, 46-47; name change, 73; public education program, 22; F. Rarig on, 22; rehabilitation center, 21-24, 35-38; W. B. Schoenbohm and, 22, 27; sheltered workshop program, 23-24; United Fund and, 38
Minnesota Spokesmen, 46-47
Minnesota State Hospital for Indigent, Crippled and Deformed Children. See Gillette Children's Hospital
Minnesota Wheelchair Sportsmen's Club, 46
Miss, John, 86
Moilanen, Mark S., 53, 68
Momoh, Lady Hannah, 103
Mooty, Melvin R., 91-92, 102
Mooty, Sally [Mrs. Melvin R.], 102
Moret, Dr. Mark, 58
Morken, Maynard, 86
Mortenson, Alice, 91, 103
Muscular Dystrophy Association, 82

Nat. G. Polinsky Rehabilitation Center, 24
National Association of Rehabilitation Facilities, 74 National Association of Rehabilitation Secretaries Service Award, 25
National Head Injury Foundation, 102
National Society for Crippled Children and Adults, 10, 21, 38, 102; Minnesota Association for Crippled Children and, 15, 21
Neal, Patricia, 99
Nees, Gerald, 98
Nelson, David, 68-69
Nemmers, Barbara, 33
Newman, Paul, 99
Nguyen, Phuonganh, 4
Nicollet Hotel (Minneapolis), 9
Nurses, 13

Oberle, Mary, 89-90
Occupational therapy, 13, 15
Ohio: disabled children, programs for, 9-10
Ohio Society for Crippled Children, 9-10
O'Laughlin, Sr. Alverna, 44

Olivia and Renville County Red Cross, 17
Olson, Chris, *99*
Olson, Gov. Floyd B., *12*-14
Olson, Helen Torgelson [Mrs. Richard R.], *18*
Olson, James S., 46-47; and Courage Residence, 51; and driver education program, 68
Olson, Richard R. "Dick," ix, *18*
Onan Foundation, 97
Onan, Robert, 97
O'Neil, Albert T., xi, 44
O'Neill, Mary Ann, *62*
Oothoudt, Tami, 62
Optimists clubs, 85
Ordway, Richard, *92*
Osmond, Donny, *99*
Osmond, Marie, *99*
Ovenshire, C. E., 9

Padilla, Donald G., *92, 104*
Palmer, Arnold, 88
Park, Les, 28
Pat Haag Memorial Endowment Fund, 89
Patterson, Kenny, *15*
Pattison, Sen. John B., *12*
Paulson, Bob, 95
Paulson, Ida, 95
Pennzoil, 88
Perfect Squares, 61
Perlman, Itzhak, 61, 73, 99, 102
Perpich, Lola [Mrs. Rudy], 99
Phillips, David A., xi, *76-78, 106-107*
Phillips, Jay, xi, 92, *101-102*
Phillips, Rose [Mrs. Jay], xi, 101-102
Phipps Foundation, 83
Phone booths, *36*
Physical therapy, 13, 17, 41
Pierce, Jean C., 21
Pillsbury Foundation, 93
Pinkham, Mary Ellen, 88
Polga, Peter, 83
Polland, Robert L., 55, 82
Pranghofer, Maureen, *44-45*
Pranghofer, Paul, 45
Public buildings, handicapped access, 35

Quiet Revolution, The (J. Haskins), 53-54
Quiggle, Dr. Arthur, *58*
Quinn, Steve, 69

Raetz, Dr., 29
Rand, Arthur, Jr., *92*
Randall, Dean B., *41, 91, 96*
Rarig, Frank M., Jr., *21*-22, 27, 91
Rashad, Ahmad, 99
Rashad, Phylicia [Mrs. Ahmad], 99
Raynor, Cynthia A., 65-67, 86
Reed, Martha, 97
Rehabilitation Act of 1973, 54
Rehabilitation centers, 21-24, 35-38, 67
Rheinberger, Max, 54

Riley, Erica, *51*
Rippe, John, 49
Robert A. and Yvonne E. MacDonald Awards, 102
Robert A. Schmitt Foundation, 66
Rochester Cowboys, 47
Rogers, Herbert, *92*
Rogers, John, 66
Roos, Jodi, *ii*
Roosevelt, Pres. Franklin D., 15
Roosevelt High School (Minneapolis, MN), 18
Rose and Jay Phillips Award, 50, 64, 75, 102
Rosemount, Inc., xi
Rotary Clubs, 9-10, 85, 90
Russ, Bob, 36-37
Ryks, Donald E., 91

Sadat, Jehan [Mrs. Anwar], *104*
St. Cloud Opportunity Training Center, 24
St. Croix National Recreation Area, 18
St. John s Landing Camp, 17-18
St. Olaf Distinguished Alumni Award, 81
St. Paul Companies Foundation, 93
St. Paul Junior League, 21
St. Paul Kiwanis Club, 18
St. Paul Opera Company, 88
St. Paul Rehabilitation Center, 21, 24
St. Paul Rolling Thunder, 47
St. Paul Schubert Club, 66
Salk, Jonas, 21
Sandness, Grace, 98
Scarlett, Ted, *87*
Schlenk, Gretchen [Mrs. Hugo, Jr.], 27
Schoenbohm, Wilko B., *xi, 41,* 49, *92,* 101-102, 112; and Camp Courage, 28; and Courage Auxiliary, 87; and Courage Center, 50; and drivers education, 68; and Minnesota Homecrafters merger, 43; biographical information, 22-23; Pat Haag on, 89; J. Houlton on, 40; National Courage Award, 102; on camping, 27; on Courage Center, xi, 74; on J. Foss, 30; on voluntary tradition, 1; retirement, 73; work, D. S. Farley on, 73-74
Scholl, Maryn, *5*
Schools: disabled children, mainstreaming, 7; disabled children, transportation, *12,* 14
Schuneman, Carl T., 91
Schuster, Gordon, 88
Schuster, Pat, 88
Schwanke, Robert, 36-37
Service Club for the Handicapped, 18
Services for the blind, 42
Shadduck, Nobel, 91-92; and Camp Courage, 27-28
Shapiro, Nathan, 89, 92

Sheltered workshops, 79
Sheltering Arms (Minneapolis, MN), 21
Sherburne-Wright County adult handicapped program, 50
Sherman, Ruth, *41*
Shriners, 9
Silverman, Robert J., 91
Silvia, Queen of Sweden, *103*
Sister Elizabeth Kenny Institute, 21
Sister Kenny Auxiliary, 64
Sister Kenny International Art Show for disabled Artists, 64
Smith, Jeanne, 73
Smith-Sears Vocational Rehabilitation Act (1919), 13
Snyder, Tom, *92*
Social Security Act, 15
Sotebeer, Marcella [Mrs. Orville], 67
Sotebeer, Orville, 67
Sound the Trumpets (movie), 36
Southwest State University (Marshall, MN), 36
Spirit of Courage, The (sculpture), 97, 101
Spivak, Marilyn Price, 102
Spurgeon Award for Achievement, 47
Stauner, Mike, 62
Steele, Richard, 44
Stokes, Karen, *28*
Storey, Ben, 98
Suel, Jay, 73
Sullivan, Kevin, 105
Sullivan, Oscar M., 9, *12*
Sunderman, Debra, *62*
Sweatt, Harold W., 32, 85, 97
Sweatt, Mary [Mrs. Harold W.], 32, 85, 97
Sweatt, William R., Jr., 32
Sweatt, William R., II, 97
Szyman, Robert J., 63, *104*

Tada, Joni Eareckson, 99, 102
Tearse, Harold, 31
Tearse, Kate Horton, 31
Tevdahl, Merlene, 68
Thayer, Rustan O., *91-92*
Thompson, Marvin, ix, 20
Thorgaard, E. K. "Bud," 27
Thorson, Frederick L., 91
3M Foundation, 83, 93
Tom Thumb Food Markets, Inc., 96
Toynbee, Arnold J., 106
Trebtoske, Julie, *60, 103*
Tributes to Courage, 73
Tufenk, Nicole, *ii*
Tuura, Carly, 54
Tuura, David, 54
Tuura, Nancy Howes [Mrs. Ronald G.], 54
Tuura, Ronald G., *54*
Twin Cities Rolling Gophers, 46-47
Twin Cities Shriners Hospital for Crippled Children, 9
Twin Cities Stroke Club, 67

Twin Ports Flyers of Duluth/Superior, 47

United Fund, 38
United States Office of Vocational Rehabilitation, 21, 36
United Way, 85, 92; Voluntary Action Center, 87
University of Minnesota, 20-21

Van Buren, Abigail, 99
Van Housen, Susan, *3*
Veith, Andrea, *80*
Veterans Bureau, 17
Veterans of Foreign Wars, 85
Vickerman, Bobbie, *60*-61
Vincent, Joyce, *23,* 50, 99
Visiting Nurse Association, 13, 42
Voigt, Mavis Amerson, xi, 87-*88,* 112
Vollhaber, Melvin P., 34, 91
Von Bodelschwingh, Dr. Friedrich, 22
Voss, Jack, 29
Voss, Judy [Mrs. Jack], 29
Vrieze, Merle, 94

Wachtler, Irma, 87
Wachtler, Raymond J., 27
Wagner, Kari, *50*
Wahlstrand, Harry, *12*
Waldschmidt, Joan, *80*
Walsh Family Foundation, 80
Walther, Francis, *29*
Warner, Janet, 88
Weiner, Jo, 89-*90*
Wendell, Lorene, 87
Wentworth, Dee, 89
West Central Industries (Willmar, MN), 24
Western Minnesota Rehabilitation and Referral Agency (Montevideo, MN), 24
Westling, Pam, *xii,* 1
Wheeler, Jean, 89
Wick, David, 39, 91
Wilichowski, Lucy, *63*
William Randolph Hearst Foundation, 88
Williams, Brittany, *87*
Williams, Theophilus Webster, *10*
Williamson, George, 43
Winona Rehabilitation Center, 24
Winther, Dr., 33
Winther, Mrs. C. P., 33
Winther Island, 33
Wirth-Davis, Michael, 79-80
Wiser, Mary, 86-87
Woltjert, Matthew, *3*
Woodland Industries (Caledonia, MN), 25
Woodward, Joanne, 99
WWII: effect on disabled, 21
Wyer, Mrs. Glenn, *12*

York, Dan I., 91
YWCA Leadership Award, 81
Zehren, Peggy [Mrs. Roger], 39
Zicarelli, Mary, *90*
Ziegler, W. H., *12*

About the author

Mavis Amerson Voigt has been associated with the Courage Center organization as staff member and volunteer since 1955, when she worked as secretary to Wilko B. Schoenbohm and later as office manager. She did volunteer work while raising a family and later worked in public relations, serving as director of the department for about five years. She is a founder of Courage Auxiliary and serves on its board of directors. Voigt, who lives in south Minneapolis, has been a free-lance writer since 1984.